First Edition

FAITH ON TRIAL BY FIRE

The Tests That You Endure In Life Are Valuable

By
Dr. Mary R. Rogers

Cover Design: Jewel V. Rogers

ISBN: 0-9726692-0-5

Additional copies of this book are available by mail.
For information on orders, please contact:

Rev. Dr. Mary R. Rogers
Miracle Revival Crusade Ministries
P.O. Box 372
Flanders, New Jersey 07836
(973) 691-9445

Printed in the United States by
Morris Publishing
3212 East Highway 30
Kearney, NE 68847
1-800-650-7888

DEDICATION

I dedicate this book to my precious mother Ella Kate Stephens. I love you for just being mother and loving me.

Love to my many sisters, brothers and other family members.

To my children, Evang. Valerie Rogers-McLendon and my son-in-law Evang. Donald McLendon for their labor of love and prayers for me. Keep up the great ministry work for the Lord.

To my son Minister Douglas Ansara Rogers, U.S. Navy and wife Jewel V. Rogers for their faith in me, and constantly reminding me to press on and complete the book.

To my younger daughter 1st Lieutenant Debra Rogers-Reese, U.S. Air Force for her financial support and encouragement. "You are a diamond in the rough for Christ".

To my son Minister Ronald McDonald and wife Lori who are precious jewels. Ronald, keep up the great music ministry of praise and worship as well as preaching the word.

To my aunts and uncles who helped to nurture me for the glory of God.

To **all** of my loving grandchildren, you are a joy and a blessing to me.

In memory of my loving grandparents, Albert Richardson, and Frances Elizabeth Richardson who taught me early to seek the Lord and love Him with all my heart.

I thank God for such loving gifts.

Acknowledgments

To my dear sister Sylvia Ann Rogers, prayer partner, armor bearer and friend, you are a jewel to me. Blessings and thanks for being there for me when I needed someone to talk to. God said you are a woman of stamina.

To Jewel my precious daughter-in-law, I am grateful for your labor of love in designing the cover for the book. Excellent job!

Special blessings and thanks to Pastor Deborah English for your laboring with me in prayer, encouragement, and answering many of my questions in writing this book for the glory of God. God said you are a gifted diamond, a precious stone.

Special thanks and blessings to Evang. Gladys Hall for your labor of love, and much support, your prayers and encouragement throughout the years.

Blessings and special thanks to Minister Kim Hall for having faith in the Christ in me. Thanks for your support and encouragement in working with me in Christ.

Special thanks to my friends Bernadette and Anthony Homer for your love and financial support towards this ministry. You are a blessing.

Special thanks and love to my mother in the Lord Alpha C. Pooler for laboring with me in proofing God's book.

Many thanks to Pastors Lawrence and Musa West, of New Jerusalem Church of Chester Inc, Chester, Pennsylvania for allowing me the opportunity to be one of your associate ministers. I have a deep love and respect for you both. You are an example to all young people and your congregation.

Finally, to Pastors Fred and Juanita Davis, of Shiloh Baptist Church, Easton, Pennsylvania thanks for your love, covering, prayers and teachings. I will never forget you.

Blessings and thanks to the many loving people, who took the time to give of their love, support, encouragement and prayers.

INTRODUCTION

Many questions are often asked as I minister to God's people; **"why is there so much suffering, and why are there so many sick and hurting people, why are we going through so much trouble, and why is this happening in my life"?** In seeking the Lord for the answer to His peoples **"whys"** and to bring healing and deliverance to His people, I began to seek Him and in seeking Him, He revealed the revelation of the **"testing"** (tribulation) His people must go through to be made righteous and ready for the Kingdom as He is coming soon.

In this writing, this author will be using paraphrases and repeated scriptures throughout the book for the **purpose** of simplicity and clarity to give understanding to God's people.

So many of God's people are led to believe that once saved they would not have to endure suffering, or go through **trying times** but Christ has already warned us that these times would come in our lives, **perilous times, testing times, dangerous times, risky times, unhealthy times and times of terror** (John 16:33 and II Timothy 3:1). Now that these times are upon us, we need to know the truth of God's word to endure and victoriously get through it (Ecclesiastes 3:1). We must also be careful not to eradicate the sufferings we must endure for Christ sake.

When we understand God's revelation of truth we will be **prepared** for any **test** that comes our way, and we can endure and stand in these times through Christ which strengthens us. God's word clearly states, "My people are destroyed **for the lack of knowledge"** (Hosea 4:6). Aren't you glad that God did not stop there, John 8:32 declares **"you shall know** the **truth** and the truth shall make you free". The prophet Hosea declares that we shall know **if** we **follow on to know** the Lord (Hosea 6:3).

The word **if** shows that a condition must be met and the condition is that you must follow on to know God's ways, and this means staying in His word, studying and living it. Knowledge comes as we follow on to know the ways of the Lord.

The Lord has revealed that "My people are suffering all kinds of **fiery trials and tribulation** because their **faith, love, obedience, character** and **works** are being put to the **test**, their **"Faith is on trial by fire"**, and I am allowing it for a Divine **purpose,"** for their good and for My glory "saith the Lord.

God requires that His people produce holiness and **the fire** will consume all that is not consistent with His holiness, (Read I Peter 4:12-13, I Corinthians 3:11-15 and Romans 8:28, Hebrews 10:27).

Job testified in his book, "when He has tried me **(tested me)**, I shall come forth as pure gold", and we know that Job suffered greatly. The word also reveals it is necessary for a **season** to be **tested** through manifold temptations **(many tests)**. We must go through, we must travail to bring forth righteousness in the earth and souls to deliverance. We suffer that others may be delivered and set free. The Apostle Paul puts it on this wise, "that we might save some". In II Corinthians 1:4 Paul reveals how God comforts us in all of our afflictions so that we will be able to comfort others who are afflicted with the same comfort which we ourselves are comforted by Him. When we go through our test and pass, we are better able to understand and help others through their time of testing.

Christ warned in I Peter 4:19 "let them that suffer according to **the will of God** commit the keeping of their souls to Him", therefore, He has assured us that we will go through things in this life. Yet God allows us to know that there is a difference in going through for His sake from going through for the sake of sin. Many in our day are suffering according to the will of God, and many are suffering because of the wages of sin, rebellion, disobedience and transgression.

There are many types of sufferings and many are going through, but the word of God promises His people in (Isaiah 43:1-2) "when you **pass through** the fire and the waters," you will not be burned (destroyed) or drowned.

You must go through the fire but **go through**, you are not to stay there. It's just a time of passing through. There is a blessing in the going through; you are being processed for a greater work, God is with you. Job went through his **test** of suffering; he went through his **fiery trials, persecution and tribulation** for a **season** and came out victorious. He did not continue in his test forever, and you will not either. He passed it, was promoted and blessed. You cannot have a testimony without a test. The test came, but it came to pass. **Job passed his test!**

You must grow up and mature in God where you can testify like Job in your testing, "though God slay me yet will I trust Him, love Him and I will maintain my ways before Him". God is looking for such faithfulness to Him in our day, that's pleasing faith. God is absolutely trustworthy, (Job 13:15). I admonish the reader to be encouraged and **go through** whatever you must go through in life and endure for Christ sake. God is with you, **"It's only a test."** The Apostle Paul shares that these light afflictions (**troubles**) are but for a moment, **a short season** (II Corinthians 4:17). You are going through but you are coming out as pure gold and that's victory.

God's eternal purpose is that each of us walk through our testing without interference or hindrance from others. It is the individual's **test**. Be careful that you do not interfere with the purpose God has ordained for one's life.

Amen

TABLE OF CONTENTS

Chapter I
TESTING, TESTING, TESTING

Profiting From The Tests In Our Lives

My brethren, count it all joy when you fall into divers temptation **(testing)**, *knowing this, that* **the trying (testing) of your faith** *worketh patience.*

But let patience have her perfect work, that you may be perfect **(mature)** *and entire, wanting (lacking) nothing.*

James 1:2-4

In order to profit from the test in your life, you must recognize that **learning experiences** comes through the **testing**. No one will escape **God's school of testing and higher learning**, we must go through, endure and graduate, as it is written we are already overcomers. This is why James admonishes; consider it pure joy, my brethren, when you face **trials of many kinds, (many tests)** because you know that the **"testing of your faith"** **develops** perseverance (endurance); Therefore, perseverance must finish its work so that you may be mature and complete, not lacking anything in any area. Perseverance is working a work in you; let it finish its course, (that you may know how to cope, how to maintain in every situation, and how to stand). Remember we must keep a right attitude and manifest good character and good behavior, when going through our test.

God wants you to know that **your testing is working for you**, its working patience in you and from the patience you can handle the **experiences** *you must go through* in life (*Romans 5:1-5*). Our experiences from the testing will produce what God wants in us **"CHARACTER"** His character, with a godly attitude. If we have God's character when we are tried, in the day of our testing, we will not be ashamed. If we have hope in Christ we are not disappointed when we are tried because the Holy Ghost, which is given unto us, pours God's love forth into our hearts and **love bears all things**. God wants us through patience to have hope.

James admonishes, blessed is the man who perseveres **(press on, stick it out)** under trial, because **when he has stood the test**, he will receive the crown of life that God has promised him. When the **test** comes in our lives it is for elevation and graduation, it is to take us higher in Christ, in growth and maturity. It also brings us into a greater anointing of power and awareness of our God, **"It's all in the TEST!"** We know that the greater the going through, the greater the anointing and manifestation of His glory. We will not graduate or come up in Him until we pass the test. God is calling us into a higher place in Him and this is where we see glory.

Blessed is the man that endureth temptation: for when he is tried, he shall receive the crown of life, which the Lord hath promised to them that love Him.

James 1:12

Our trials **(tests)** and **tribulations** are inevitable. If you need wisdom concerning what Christ is accomplishing in your life through the trials, ask Him "Lord what am I to learn in this test"? Know that God has a divine **purpose** in every test in your life, it is a promise, **life is a series of tests**. The Word admonishes; **"you shall have them"!**

Listen to the voice of Jesus, "These things I have **warned** you of, that in Me you might have peace. In this world, **you shall have tribulation (testing)**. You will **go through** many things in this life but be of good cheer; I have overcome the world." God wants **you** to know that the victory of any **test** is **your knowing** that **you can overcome** through Christ. In crisis times and even what you may be going through at this very moment, **you** are an overcomer through Christ who loves you.

2

Testing, Testing, Testing

These things I have spoken unto you, that in Me you might have peace. In the world you shall have tribulation: but be of good cheer; I have overcome the world.

John 16:33

Your Test Is Working For You

Our trials and testing are causing **(conformity)** to God's word, **which will produce character**. They are working for our good according to *Romans 8:28-29*.

The **purpose** of testing is to strengthen our character, produce comforters to the body of Christ and cause us to have a deeper commitment to God; it also causes us to wait for His perfect **timing** in whatever His will is for our lives. God knows what lies ahead and we must be tried, we must be prepared, we must go through for His name's sake.

To everything there is a season, and a time to every purpose under the heaven...

Ecclesiastes 3:1

When God says **"all things"** work together for our good, He means just that, your testing, hurting, rejection and sufferings are a part of God's redemptive grace for a testimony to bring someone else into the kingdom, unto salvation and deliverance. You have been called into the Kingdom for such. **Fear not!**

And we know that all things work together for good to them that love God, to them who are the called according to His purpose.

Romans 8:28

Hear the words of the Lord Jesus concerning your trials and sufferings...

*"For as much then as Christ have suffered for us in the flesh, **arm yourselves likewise** with the same mind: for he that has suffered in the flesh has ceased **from sin**;*

I Peter 4:1

That he no longer should live the rest of his time in the flesh to the lusts of men, but to the will of God.

I Peter 4: 2

Your suffering is working for you; the test is good for you! The Apostle Paul addresses the church in Thessalonica and he reveals to them how God uses our sufferings to make us worthy of His kingdom.

We are bound to thank God always for you, brethren, as it is meet, because that your faith groweth exceedingly, and the charity of every one of you all toward each other aboundeth;

II Thessalonians 1:3

So that we ourselves glory in you in the churches of God, for your patience and faith in all your persecutions and tribulations that you endure:

II Thessalonians 1:4

Which is a manifest token of the righteous judgment of God that you may be counted worthy of the kingdom of God, for which you also suffer...

II Thessalonians 1:5

Remember, Christ in His humanity endured bodily **sufferings and testing**. He suffered physical and mental anguish, and the prophets and disciples of old went through also. You can also through Christ endure the same *(Matthew 5:12)*. He will never *allow* you to face a **test** that you cannot overcome without offering or giving you a way of escape. **He will give you a way to pass the test** and when you pass, His glory is revealed. God is faithful!

God's word encourages us that Christ has suffered being **tested**, and was tried by suffering. Since He felt the pain of trials and temptations, He is able to **quickly deliver** His children being tempted, **tested** and tried as He has promised "I come quickly for My elect's sake". We have an open invitation as His children to come *boldly* to His throne of grace, that we may obtain mercy and find His grace to help us in needy times, **testing times**, times of terror, persecution, **tribulation** and affliction.

For we have not an High Priest which cannot be touched by the feeling of our infirmities; but was in all points tempted like we are, yet without sin.

Hebrews 4:15

The Lord spoke to my spirit saying, "prophesy My daughter, **tell My people it is testing time. I am testing, testing, testing. The hour of testing is come, testing has come upon ALL saith the Lord,** and it will intensify as time progresses; tell them that their faith and lives will be tested". God said, "hold on, don't loose or lose your courage, don't faint; Behold, I come quickly, hold fast to that which you have, that no man take your crown."

Because you have kept the word of my patience, I also will keep you from the hour of temptation, which shall come upon all the world, to try them that dwell upon the earth.

Behold, I come quickly: hold that fast which you have, that no man take your crown.

Revelation 3:10-11

He that has an ear let him hear what the Spirit saith unto the churches.

Revelation 3:13

Hearken unto this prophecy; Fear none of those things God said which you shall suffer, **fear not the test or the tribulation**, don't be afraid. Satan is about to throw some of you into prison or prison situations to have your **faith and life tested** for a short season, hold on to your faith, don't let go. God said it's **"only a test!"** **I warn you,** "it won't always be easy, but I will be with you saith the Lord".

*Fear **none** of those things, which you shall **suffer**: behold, the devil shall cast some of you into **prison**, that you may be **tried**; and you shall have **tribulation** ten days: be thou faithful unto death, and I will give you a crown of life.*

Revelation 2:10

From Whence Cometh Temptations

James explicitly warned when speaking of the sources of temptation, that no one should say, "God is tempting me" **(alluring or enticing one to sin or evil)**. For God cannot be tempted by evil, nor does He tempt anyone; but each one is tempted when he is drawn away **by focusing and yielding to his own evil desire**.

6

It is not the temptation but the yielding that causes one to sin, then, after desire has conceived, it gives birth to sin; and sin, when it is full-grown brings forth death. (Paraphrased)

Let no man say when he is tempted, I am tempted of God: for God cannot be tempted with evil, neither tempteth He any man:

James 1:13

But every man is tempted, when he is drawn away of his own lust, and enticed.

James 1:14

Then when lust have conceived, it bringeth forth sin: and sin, when it is finished, bringeth forth death.

James 1:15

The **Greek** term translated **"tempted"** can also be translated **"tested"**. **Massah** is a name that means, **"testing or tempting."** When Israel was tested during the time of their wilderness experiences their response to testing was not that of obedience and trust to God many times. God proved Israel in the wilderness. God does not tempt us but He will surely allow us to be tested in areas of our lives.

You shall not tempt the Lord your God, as you tempted Him in Massah.

Deuteronomy 6:16

Adam and Eve were **tested** in the garden. Watch this, *"the tree test"*...

7

When warned, "but the tree of the knowledge of **good and evil**", **do not eat** for in the day you eat, you shall *surely* die. Adam and Eve yielded to the trickery, lie and lust of satan, gave birth to their desires and brought forth the fruit of sin and death. *Disobedience caused them not to pass the test.* God **only** wanted them to know good, not evil.

God knew the evil that was on the tree, He knew what was on the tree that would lead one to sin and death. Satan tempted them, but God tested them to see if they would obey, and **they failed the test**.

God gave them a choice. God gives us choices also in our day and it is up to us to make the right choice, and that choice is obedience. God proves **(test)** us to see if we will obey Him.

And the Lord God took the man, and put him into the Garden of Eden to dress it and to keep it.

Genesis 2:15

And the Lord God commanded the man saying, of every tree of the garden thou may freely eat:

Genesis 2:16

But of the tree of the knowledge of good and evil, thou shall not eat of it: for in the day that you eat thereof you shall surely die.

Genesis 2:17

Temptation comes from within one's inner thoughts, disposition or character and feeds on the attractions of sin. For our understanding, **temptation** can be defined as evil thoughts, drawn away through strong imaginations, lust, and enticement, **yielding** to lust, sinful acts committed, and death as its result.

Tribulation can be defined as a trying **experience, affliction, suffering** and **persecution**. Wrongdoing and oppression are other testing words, these are all spokes in the same wheel meaning synonymously the same, they are related words.

Testing comes from without, and is an outside force with which one has no control over *(Job had no control over his test but he could surely resist the temptation of sinning against God).* You to can **choose** not to yield to sinning against God. God is not the source of temptation. God did not tempt Adam and Eve. He tested them.

The Greek word for **trial** is **peripipto,** to fall into, to be caught by. The Greek word for different trials is **peirasmos**: which means *to try, trial, put to proof,* examine or question.

Do You Really Want To Be Like Jesus?

Often we testify that we want to be like Jesus, yet there are some things concerning Jesus' ministry we do not want to experience. There are **tests** that He went through that we fear enduring such as spiritual nails, thorns and (gall) a bitter cup, and what about sorrows, **rejection**, being despised, and being acquainted with grief? He was spat upon, lied on, misunderstood and forsaken; humiliated and denied. He was even called a false prophet. All of these are *sufferings* of Christ that many of God's people do not want to endure. **Rejection** is one of the most trying *tests* of our day. Rejection hurts and yet we see here that Christ was rejected.

I say to those of you that are hurting today and feeling rejected and unloved; and you feel as if no one cares, Jesus cares! He cares for you, He loves you! He's been where you are in your hurts, rejection and trials, your sufferings and temptations.

He is mindful of what you are going through at this very moment. **"You can make it!"**

*He is despised and **rejected** of men; a man of sorrows, and acquainted with grief: and we hid as it were **our faces from Him**; He was despised, and we esteemed Him not.*

Isaiah 53:3

Remember, the hurts He bore for us! He has revealed that we have a High Priest who is touched by the feelings of our infirmities (weakness of flesh). We have One who has been **tested** in all points (all areas of life) as we ourselves are now tested". He bore in **"all things"** the likeness of our trials, yet He did not sin. He has been where you are!

For we have not an high priest which cannot be touched with the feelings of our infirmities; but was in all points tempted like as we are, yet without sin.
Hebrews 4:15

Now that you have heard the testimony of His **test**, "do you still want to be like Jesus? I pray you said **yes**! He **is** our example. You can flow with Him. He can take you victoriously through anything.

Be Encouraged

It encourages us to know that God does not renege on His promises, He is not negligent according to mans conception, but He patiently deals with each of us to bring us to repentance and salvation, you can **trust Him in your testing**, He is absolutely trust worthy. I encourage you today while many are going through the fire of affliction, suffering in many ways, not sure if they are coming through or out of the *test*, God is faithful to bring you out and to give you an expected end.

Testing, Testing, Testing

*The Lord is not slack concerning His promise, as some men count slackness; but is **longsuffering** to us-ward, not willing that any should perish but that all should come to repentance.*

II Peter 3:9

God knows how much you can take. It is more than you could imagine, through Christ.

Okay, it's time for a praise break...let us stop and give Him thanks right now for our promised victory. Hallelujah, hallelujah, hallelujah! Praise the name of the Most High God!

Father I thank you that "I will go through victoriously through Christ, He will not leave me or forsake me in this test". I am not alone.

Remember, He did not forsake Adam and Eve when they went through their *test* in the Garden of Eden. He made provision for them even though they failed to pass the *test*. He did not leave Daniel when he was in his den of *testing*. He did not leave Shadrach, Meshach, and Abed-Nego in their *fiery* testing. He did not leave Joseph when his brothers persecuted and sold him and threw him into his pit of *testing*. He did not forsake or leave Father Abraham when he was *tested* to sacrifice his only son promised of God. He did not leave or forsake the Apostle Paul in his many *testings*. God will not forsake you. To give you another key, God did not forsake or leave His son when He had gone through divers *testings* for His Bride (you and me), when His **testing** was over God received Him, He returned to His Father.

When Jesus was tested on the cross God could not even look on His only begotten Son because of the darkness of our sins He bore in His own body, but when it was finished, Jesus cried out with a loud voice and said "Father into Thy hands I commend My spirit: and having said thus, He gave up the ghost.

11

I can almost hear Him saying; "Father I have fought a good fight, I have completed My work and I'm coming back home to You." He had obeyed and completed His earthly mission that His Father had sent Him to accomplish. I could go on and on with these great testimonies of encouragement. I want you to know that He is and will be with you also; He will never leave or forsake you. You too can finish the work He has sent you to do; you can finish your course. Amen

Different Trials Come

What are **trials**? They are what we encounter or go through in life, our battles, struggles and **sufferings**. They are a state of pain or anguish that **tests** one's **resiliency and character**. It is something hard to bear physically or emotionally. It is also called tribulation. A trial is a temptation or adversity, the enduring of which **proves** our faith to be true or false. *Many positive things are manifested through our trials.* God does not exempt believers from difficult circumstances, He **tests** the righteous and the wicked (Psalms 11:5).

Let us consider some different trials manifested in the word. There are **suffering tests, which** are trials believers may be called upon to *go through and endure* as seen with the servant Job and the Apostle Paul. There are many other biblical servants that suffered also.

"For I will show him (Paul) how great things he must suffer for My name's sake".

Acts 9:16

We are admonished of **the persecution test** in *(Matthew 5:11-12)* Blessed are you when men shall revile you, (abuse, denounce and give you a bad name) **persecute** you, hurt you, and

12

shall say all manner of evil against you falsely, *"for My name's sake."* God said you are blessed when these things happen to you. He also *forewarned* us that these times would come, that persecution and troublesome times would come, that times of terror and adversity would come.

God wants us to be joyful and triumphant in our *trials* and *testing*, because we have a great reward in heaven. There is a great cloud of witnesses, the *prophets* and servants of old who have gone on before us, who were tried and *tested* in like manner and they were counted happy that endured, and they obtained a **good report** wherein we call them the Heroes of Faith. This is an inspired example for us.

Take, my brethren, the prophets, who have spoken in the name of the Lord, for **an example** *of suffering affliction, and of patience. Behold we count them happy which endure...*

James 5:10-11

The love test: When they had eaten breakfast, Jesus said to Simon Peter, "Simon, son of Jonah, do you *love* Me more than these?" (God wants our love for Him to exceed anything or anyone). Simon said to Jesus, "Yes, Lord; You know that I love You." Jesus said to him, "Feed My lambs." Jesus said to Peter again **a second time**, "Simon, son of Jonah, do you love Me?" Peter said to Jesus, "Yes, Lord You know that I love You." Jesus said to him, "Tend to My sheep." Jesus said to Peter **a third time**, "Simon, son of Jonah, do you love Me?" Peter was grieved because Jesus said to him **a third time**, "Do you love Me?" And he said to Him, "Lord, You know all things, You know that I love You." Jesus said to him "Feed My sheep". Sometimes God has to speak His word to us again and again until it gives birth to our spirit, until reality comes alive, and then we know, that we know, that we know that God means business with us.

13

God often says in His word **"again I say unto you"**, He will repeat it again and again until you get it, until your spirit man receives it.

Do you think Peter might have been fearful of another **test** coming his way, and of not passing it as with his denial of Christ? Do you think that he was afraid that this would lead to another failed test? Was this the reason he was so irritated at the questions? Know that we are **tested** to reveal our love, faith, trust, character and humility, that Christ might be glorified. It's in enduring and passing our test that Jesus is glorified.

Sometimes we think that we know so much about ourselves, more than Christ does, but after a failed *test* and repentance, we find out that we really don't know ourselves at all. This we do know though that after a humbling experience, a humbling *test*, we can be sure that we love Jesus. He wanted Peter to be sure of his love and his answer. He wanted him to have a right focus and clarity of purpose. Christ is asking His people the same question today at this time, *"do you love Me more than anything or anyone?"*

He is commanding us to feed His people the word of God, to care for them and love them, both the lambs (little ones) and His sheep (the older ones). We must have a nurturing spirit!

The hatred test: Christ *warned* us that we would be hated of **all nations**, and we are seeing that manifestation in our world today. Hate is all around us and this will continue to be the attitude of the world until Jesus comes. God's word declared that evil men would wax worse and worse. People of God you will be hated because of your love for Christ, because your deeds are good and not evil. The world will hate you because of Christ's glory in you, His light in you uncovers their darkness, their sins.

Jesus exhorts His body, marvel not *(don't be surprised)*, my brethren, if the world hates you, they hated Me first.

He also warned us not to hate our brethren because whosoever hateth his brother is a murderer. Therefore, we as Christians must love not only our brothers but everybody, even our enemies.

You shall be hated of all men for My name's sake, but he that endureth to the end shall be saved.
Matthew 10:22

Whosoever hateth his brother is a murderer: and you know that no murderer has eternal life abiding in him.

1 John 3:15

When God says whosoever, that's a good place to insert your name, "if _____ hates (his/her) brother or sister (he/she) is a murderer". It's God's word, **"it is written"**.

Abraham's test of faith, obedience and works: And it came to pass after these things, that God did tempt **(test, proved)** Abraham, and said to him Abraham, and Abraham answered, Behold here I am. And God said to him, take now thy son, *your only son* Isaac *whom you love*, and go into the land of Moriah; and offer him there for a burnt offering upon one of the mountains, that I will tell you of, and Abraham obeyed.

During the time of preparation for the sacrifice, Isaac spoke to Abraham his father and said, "My father," and he said, "Here I am, my son." Then he said, "Look, the fire and the wood but where is the lamb for a burnt offering, where is the lamb for the sacrifice?" And Abraham said, "My son, God will provide for Himself the lamb for a burnt offering". (Paraphrased) We see father and son being tested.

Isaac is being **tested** here also as a little boy. Often times we forget that each of us has our own tailor-made **test** ordered. God's little children are not exempt from being tested; their *test* is just written differently, they must be **proven** also.

15

The child Isaac obeyed God also by obeying his father Abraham. Isaac did not put up any resistance of rebellion but *yielded* to obedience. For the bible declares, "train up a child in the way it should go, and with that training comes testing.

> *Train up a child in the way he should go, and when he is old, he will not depart from it.*

> Proverbs 22:6

> *Remember now Thy Creator in the days of thy youth...*

> *Ecclesiastes 12:1*

Some **tests** are for **examples** but all *tests* are for **purpose**. In his **test**, the Bible states that Abraham stretched out his hand and took the knife to slay *his only son*. But the Angel of the Lord called to him from heaven and said, "Abraham, Abraham", and he said, "here I am." And he said, "Do not lay your hand on the boy, or do anything to him; for **now I know that you fear God, since you have not withheld your son, your only son, from Me.**" God said, don't do it son, it's only a test! (What a **test**, what a testimony). **"It was only a test!"** God offered Abraham and Isaac a way of escape for there was a ram caught in a thicket behind him and Abraham took the ram and offered it up for a brunt offering **instead of his son**. Praise God for your ram in the bush, your way of escape when you think you are **tested** above measure. Remember God is faithful; He will always offer you a way of escape. The passing of Abraham's **test** pleased God so, He said to Abraham, by Myself have I sworn that because you have done this thing (you have trusted and obeyed Me), and **have not withheld** your son, your only son; in blessing I will bless you, and in multiplying I will multiply your seed as the stars of the heaven, and as the sand which is upon the sea shore; and your seed (children and offspring) shall possess the gate of your enemies and in your seed shall all the nations of the earth be blessed; **because you obeyed My Voice**. Aren't you grateful we are Abraham's seed, the righteous seed of God? **It pays to yield and obey His Voice!**

People of God we must remember that anything we love and hold dear to us more than God, needs to be placed on the altar, it needs to be burned and nothing left but the ashes to remind you not to go that way again. If your test has not already come, **it will**, to see where your love and your heart lie. Our God is a jealous God!

God promises that He will not allow us to be **tested** or tempted above what we are able to bear. **Oh this is a good place for you to stop reading and praise Him**. Hallelujah, I love You Lord, I adore You, I Praise Your Holy name!

Jehovah-jireh will also provide for you in any given situation or circumstance a way of escape if you obey Him. Remember, after **passing the test**, you are graded and rewarded abundantly. There are an abundance of blessings waiting to be manifested to you (Read Genesis 22:1-18). God is faithful!

The hardship test: It is necessary that you go through your hardship **test** for this is the time when adversity and tribulation is used as a tool to mature us. God will bring you through the fire and through the waters. He is to be and will be regarded in our afflictions. Know that God has a divine purpose in every trial and suffering that you endure.

Man that is born of a woman is of few days and full of trouble.

Job 14:1

17

Yet man is born unto trouble, as the sparks fly upward.

Job 5:7

Listen to the testimony of King David..."**Before** I was **afflicted** I went astray: **but now** have I kept Thy word". I believe that David was saying, "I used to wander off and do my own thing until You chastened me and I went through some hardships in life; now I will follow You closely and do what You command. David further testifies, *"It is good for me that I have been afflicted* (**tried, tested, proven, chastened**) **that I might learn** Thy statutes." David was a man after God's own heart yet he too had a lesson to learn through adversity. We too have lessons to learn.

It is good for me that I have been afflicted; that I might learn Thy statues. I know, O Lord, that Thy judgments are right, and that You in faithfulness have afflicted me.

Psalm 119:71,75

David attributed his affliction to God, he did not say as many confess today, "Oh the loving God would not afflict His people, the loving God would not allow His leader to go through this or that. He did not eradicate the chastening of the Lord as many do today. Many today, when things happen say it's the devil, the devil, the devil; it is not always the devil on your case. Listen to David a man after God's own heart...He confessed, it is good that "**You**" afflicted me; I can learn something from this. Your judgments are right Lord; **You have afflicted** me in Your faithfulness. We have eradicated God's chastening and judgments for so long that there is little fear of God in the earth. God is a God of Love, but you need to flip the coin and see His other side. He is also a God of judgment and wrath. Don't deceive yourself! God is not mocked. God's word is sure.

Testing, Testing, Testing

In the book of II Samuel, Chapter 11 the story is told of the test David went through and the results of not passing the **test** when we know God's word and warnings.

Watch this! King David after the year ended, at the time when kings went forth to battle, sent Joab and his servant with him and all Israel to war, but David remained at Jerusalem in his royal palace. At sunset he got up from his couch, walked to the roof of his palace and saw a beautiful woman bathing.

Watch the test, the temptation here... He sent for her, went to bed with her, got her pregnant and tried to cover it up. I can understand why the songwriter warns, "Yield Not To Temptation, for *Yielding is Sin*". David *yielded* to the lust of sin through his eyes, and his emotions, was enticed and seduced by satan. Remember, it was the eyes that got Eve in trouble, the same satanic trick. **Our eyes and our emotions can lead us into the same satanic trap today.** Lust was conceived, and gave birth to adultery, conception, an evil device, treachery, murder and then death. David committed adultery with a woman whom he had already been warned had a husband. He was informed that she was the wife of Uriah, one of his men of war, one of his servants. We see that David, God's servant did not heed the **warning (the way of escape),** which was sent to prepare him to pass the test. In not heeding, he failed the test wherein, if he had only listened, he could have passed it. God will always warn us before a failed test, before destruction comes.

After David had done this evil, he tried to set Uriah up by encouraging him to sleep with his wife Bathsheba. This was so that David could cover up the wrong he had done. But God gave Uriah wisdom, self-control, a restrained sexual appetite, and a way of escape. These were Uriah's words to King David, "The Ark, Israel, and Judah, abide in tents; and my lord Joab, and the servants of my lord are camped in the open field; shall I go into my house to eat, drink and have pleasure with my wife?

As thou live, and as thy soul live, I will not do this thing. Uriah said, "I will not do it!" Still trying to cover his sin, David sends Uriah to the front lines where the war was intense and left him there that he might get killed. What an evil, cruel thing to do to one of your servants, especially one that serves, watches and protects you in battle, one that has your best interest at heart. The message went back to David that "thy servant Uriah the Hittite is dead," and when the wife of Uriah heard that her husband was dead, she mourned for him and when the mourning was ended, oh yes, there is a time when all mourning comes to an end. David sent for her and she became his wife and she bare him the son conceived in sin and iniquity. David failed this **test**, and God was displeased with David's evil actions.

When we fail our testing we cause others to go through great battles, sometimes unnecessary battles. David brought tribulation (family trouble) upon his entire household, the Bible says, forever. Hear the word of the Lord sent to David through the prophet... And the Lord sent Nathan the prophet unto David saying, "wherefore, have you despised the commandments of the Lord to do evil in His sight"? **Look at God's uncovering here. Don't ever think that God does not see us when we are in our mess,** "You have killed Uriah the Hittite with the sword, taken his wife to be your wife, and have slain him by the sword of the children of Ammon". Now therefore, the sword (trouble, hardship) shall *never* depart from your house, (your family) *because you have despised Me*, and have taken the wife of Uriah the Hittite to be your wife". Notice, God **did not** give David this wife, it was David's choice out of lust and treachery.

Please bear in mind that this was not a marriage ordained in heaven by God, it was birthed out of lust sin and adversity therefore, it brought forth death. This sin caused the death of Bathsheba's husband Uriah and the death of the child that Uriah's wife bore unto David.

20

People of God, know that there are penalties and consequences for disobedience and sin for the saved and sinner alike. God hates sin and when we sin we fall under His chastening, judgments and wrath. God in His sovereignty will not allow us to go unpunished for our sins and trespasses. If you think so you are highly deceived. His prophetic words to David was "Behold, I **will raise up evil against you** out of your own house, and I will take your *wives* before your eyes, and give them to your neighbor, in the sight of this sun". God warned David, you did this thing secretly, but I will uncover you before all Israel, and before the sun." I will uncover you and bring it to the light *(II Samuel 12:11-12). Know that what you do in the dark will always come to the light.*

Repentance Is The Prerequisite For Forgiveness

David confessed his sins and turned from them and God forgave him. David had a powerful testimony after his hardship and testing. **Read it!** *(Psalm 51 and Psalm 119:65-76)* His testimony of God's forgiveness and mercy encourage us today.

After every **test if passed** comes victory, promotion, restoration and blessings. God is saying to His people now come higher, *pass your test* and "come up in Me". God is calling us to a higher place in Him, a higher and new realm in His Spirit.

God wants us to come into a place in Him where we recognize that we are going through a *test*, know that it is ordained for us and come above it without murmuring and complaining. He wants us to soar like the eagle in the things of God. The testing will produce the obedience and approved character of God expected of us. God has revealed that many come in His name but few in His character. It's time to mature!

21

God Wants Us To Know Our Heart

Our testing leads us sometimes into a **difficult** way for **purpose**. When God revealed to Israel their **test** of humility and obedience these were His words to them, "you shall remember all the way which the Lord your God led you these forty years in the wilderness, *to humble you, and prove* (test) *you*, **to know what was in your heart, whether you would keep His commandments or not"**. God knows your heart, but the **test** is for you to be assured that you will love Him and keep His commandments. You have got to know that you know, that you know that you will love and obey Him no matter what the test.

God brought His people by *a difficult way* to humble them, and He is doing the same in our day. **You** must know what's in **your** heart! He is *testing* us that He might uncover our true disposition and **character**. *He writes the test*! The Apostle Paul admonishes us to *endure* **hardship** as a good soldier. He is indicating the opposition, difficulty, injuriousness and trouble we must endure. God's grace is sufficient for our endurance in hardship testing. The tests reveal our heart and motives under pressure if we will obey God.

*Thou therefore **endure hardness**, as a good soldier of Jesus Christ.*

II Timothy 2:3

Whatever you must go through, pass the test! Go through!

There Is A Test Designed For Every One

When your time of divers testing comes, remember God has forewarned us to think it not strange. We should not be surprised when we suffer, "the godly in Christ will suffer".

He warned us that; **perilous times**, troublesome times, difficult times, times of crisis, times of **"stress"** and **hardship** would come, and the times will be dangerous. The times are here, these are the last days, the end time. Suffering times are here, God said, *"testing, testing, testing"*.

> *This know also, that in the last days perilous times shall come.*

> *II Timothy 3:1*

Again, I remind you **"the hour of testing**, the times of testing will come upon the **whole world to try them"** (Revelation 3:10). Can you see the handwriting on the wall when you look at the things that are going on in our world today?

God is trying to get His people's attention as He did in the days of Noah and in the days of Lot before it's too late, before His judgment and wrath comes. There are many people, many noble and even many preachers and leaders in the church that are not listening. Repent and believe the gospel. **This is a wake up call to all**!

Matthew 26:41 forewarns us to "watch and pray, that we enter not into temptation because the spirit indeed is willing to obey God, but *our flesh is weak"*. Jesus is warning us to watch ourselves and pray that we may be spared in the time of testing and the prerequisite for sparing us is repent, turn from our own wicked ways, receive forgiveness and help others. Can you see God's Word living in our world today?

Everyone has a **test**, it's just written differently. God knows how much and what we can bear. He knows our testing ability. He has also given us what we need to pass every test. He has given us His precious Holy Spirit to lead and guide us through whatever test or task we must endure.

23

Testing is *needful* to build our obedience and faith in God that it be found *genuine* and thus to be rewarded. Our faith will be proven by trials, as we have seen with David's testimony *(Psalm 119:71-75)*. David reveals the affliction **(the test)** was necessary. It showed David areas in his life that needed deliverance and that he needed to trust God in. Isn't it amazing how we can believe and have faith in God to save us from everything but our sex drive, and sexual appetites? We don't believe that God can handle that. He **CAN** handle it, He will help you to abstain, trust Him, and you will be surprised! This is the greatest area of testing in our lives today. This is an area where satan has intensified and released his ungodliness against all of humanity. We need to submit and commit our sex drive to Christ. He is able to keep all that you commit to Him until He is ready to release you in marriage for His glory. The piercing in His side took care of our inordinate affections and lust.

Our *testing* comes for learning experiences and there are great blessings and rewards for our testing.

Blessed is the man that endureth temptation: for when he is tried, he shall receive the crown of life, which the Lord hath promised to them that love Him.
James 1:12

Christians and sinners alike will be tried **(tested)**. People of God, know that when trouble comes, when **tribulation** comes, it will work righteousness in us. Like things comes upon all, we are all being **tested**, and it might sound like bad news, but it is really good news as it will propel us to our destiny.

The Apostle Paul admonishes in *(Acts 14:22)* we cannot enter the Kingdom of heaven without **many trials, much testing**. – We will enter through much tribulation, persecution, affliction, hardship and troubles. God's word is true, it is not going to change **we** must change!

God has given us how to pass our test and to get through these difficult times. He warns, "Believe the Gospel!" Repent!

Listen to the *parable of the sower*... "But he that received the seed (the word of God) into stony places, the same is he that hears the word, and right away receives it with *joy but it takes no real root in him*. He lives the word for a little while but when *suffering*, persecution and the **(testing)** come, because of the Word, he backslides and turns his back on Christ. He cries out, "I can't take it any more" and goes back to his old ways. Don't turn from Christ, that's the time to turn whole heartily **to** Him and therefore endure your test. **He will help you**.

In **Joseph's test**, he was sold for a servant, his feet were hurting in chains, he was bound in iron *(testing)*, until the **time** that the word came, **and the word tested him**. Two **keys** are evident here in his testing, *timing* and the *word*.

On God's prophetic time clock, "To everything there is a **time and a season**".

To everything there is a season, and a time to every purpose under the heavens...
Ecclesiastes 3:1

As for God, His way is perfect: the word of the Lord is tried.

Psalm 8:30

You see, God only allowed his afflictions, persecutions and testing for a moment, *for a season*. God will never allow you to be tested or tried above what you can stand; He just will not allow it! **Remember, you cannot have a testimony without a test**.

Joseph's faith in the word of God regarding his dreams was severely tested. Even while he was in chains in prison, he seemed never to have (wavered) in God's Divine revelation and purpose for his life *(Genesis 37:5-10).*

After Joseph's *test,* after his season of going through, and after his captivity came victory, freedom and blessings. "The King sent and **loosed him** and even the ruler let him go **free**".

Joseph's testing and afflictions elevated him from the pit to the palace and before a great king that God had ordained and would use to be the very blessing and fulfillment of his dreams. God will always work out what you are going through for your good. After Joseph had passed his **test** of the pit and other testing, this was his testimony to his brothers; the same ones he had testified to of his dreams and that had persecuted him...

But as for you, you thought evil against me; but God meant it unto good, to bring to pass, as it is this day, to save much people alive.

Genesis 50:20

Now therefore, fear you not; I will nourish you, and your little ones, and he comforted them, and spake kindly unto them.

Genesis 50:21

This is God's salvation plan even for His people in our day; we too must go through our **test**, our sufferings, and tribulations and endure, so that we can save much people alive. God saved us to help save others; we go through for the sake of other's salvation. Sometimes you will have to go through and endure your pit situations, which is your **test** to bring forth souls and to help others. When your pit seems so dark and it seems that you are never coming out, in shines the Light and lifts you to your destiny for His glory. Out of great tests come great testimonies.

God is always with you helping you to pass every test. After we have suffered and passed the test, we can come rejoicing bringing in a harvest of souls into the kingdom of God. Joseph did!

Remember, where there are no tests there are no testimonies. You cannot have a testimony without a test!

Chapter II

JUDGMENT, THE TEACHER

He is the Lord our God: His judgments are in all the earth.
Psalm 105:7

The way of the just is uprightness: Thou, Most Upright, do weigh the path of the just.
Isaiah 26:7

Yes, in the way of Your judgments, O Lord, have we waited for You; the desire of our soul is to Your name, and to the remembrance of You.
Isaiah 26:8

A Lesson To Learn

With my soul have I desired You in the night; yes with my spirit within me will I seek You early: "for **when Your judgments are in the earth, the inhabitants of the world will learn righteousness***.*
Isaiah 26:9

"God's judgments will produce the kind of righteousness He is expecting and looking for in the earth. His people will learn to live right by His standards".

God said when favor is shown to the wicked, they still will not learn to do right: in the land of honesty they will deal unjustly, and will not see the majesty of the Lord. The wicked man though spared does not learn fairness or righteousness; they do not regard the ways of God. His heart is not to do what is right in the sight of the Lord or His people. Nevertheless, God declares that their own wickedness shall correct them and their backsliding will reprove them. But Grace says, "let the wicked forsake his way and turn unto God who will abundantly pardon".

28

Lord, when Your hand is lifted up, they will not see: but they shall see, and be ashamed for their envy at the people, yes, the fire of Thine enemies shall devour them.

Isaiah 26:11

God's hand is lifted up in judgment even now. God is revealing in this hour that many of His people have committed evils; they have forsaken Him and **turned** their backs on Him. Jeremiah the prophet declares that, "As the thief is ashamed when he is caught in the act (the act of sin), so is the house of Israel (God's people) ashamed; they, their kings **(leaders)**, their **princes**, their **priests**, and their **prophets**", saying to a stock **(their idol god)**, you are my father; and to a stone, you have brought me forth (you have blessed me): "for they have turned their back unto Me, and not their face saith the Lord". But **in the time of their trouble they will say, arise, and save us.**

There is just something about tribulation   **(testing)** that will cause one to cry out to God, **save me!** This shows us that tribulation is necessary for God's people will not cry out any other way. Many will not acknowledge Him any other way. Many are like Jeshurun; they get fat off of God's blessing and prosperity and forsake Him, they soon forget Him. Know that when you do this, it will lead you into tribulation (trouble).

*Lord, in **trouble (testing times, in times of distress)** have they visited You, they poured out a prayer when Your chastening was upon them.*
Isaiah 26:16

Some people will not even think about God until trouble and disaster hits, and at that time, even the atheist and the non-believer will cry out "Lord have mercy".

God's message to Hezekiah in the Old Testament is still the same message to us today... This is your **News Brief**— **"Hear ye, hear ye, this is a day of trouble, rebuke and blasphemy**; for the children (souls) need to be birthed, and there is no strength to bring them forth". God is giving you a picture of the times we are in and what is going on in the world today, this is our daily news. He is also letting you know that He knows what is going on. He wants souls to be saved, delivered and set free, He wants them to be born again and enter the Kingdom of God. "For He came to set the captive free." Many today are not being delivered and made free.

The Word declares, "we have been with child (pregnant in spirit), we have been in pain (gone through much), and we have as it were brought forth wind; we have **"NOT"** brought forth any deliverance in the earth; neither have the inhabitants (souls) of the world fallen. Many have miscarried their births with religiosity (the traditions of man) and self-gratification. It is the Word of God that gives life, which gives birth.

We have yet to see the ministry of Jesus Christ and the disciples manifested in our day. It is time for God's love to come to the forefront in His people by our example. Many are looking for the **manifestation** of the sons of God; they are looking for Christ in us the hope of glory, those that profess salvation that profess to be born again and delivered. God's people are looking to see the greater works promised to us by Jesus working in and through us. Many expect to see signs, wonders, miracles, and souls saved and delivered following them and so does Christ. The world is looking for the real Christ, a Living Savior, the One who lives in us by example as in the disciples of old. We can show them through the Holy Spirit, through Christ that He is alive today.

It is time for the body of Christ to travail in birth and bring forth **righteousness by example**, so that we can bring forth souls. "Truly the harvest is ready, the fields are ripe to glean" and God does not want us to let this harvest pass. We have been pregnant in spirit for a long time. **Now** it's time for birth "saith the Lord".

As The Days Of Noah

But as the days of Noah were, so shall also the coming of the Son of Man be (Matthew 24:37).

In Noah's day, God had to send forth His judgments, tribulation and destruction because of the transgressions, wickedness and sins of His people. We see the same pattern in the world today. For God has already forewarned us that there shall be great tribulation (testing, trials, persecution and afflictions) such as was not since the beginning of the world because of sin.

I have warned you that false christs, and false prophets will arise showing great signs and wonders and **if it were possible** they would fool the very elect of God. "Behold, I have told you before" *(Matthew 24:25). My elect has been warned, saith the Lord.* Make sure that you are not running after signs and wonders but after the Lord Jesus Christ and His word of **truth and righteousness**; for satan will be manifesting lying signs and wonders, his influential seductive activities as in times past. His nature is always to counterfeit what Jesus commands and to confuse us by his evil works.

Remember Moses' rod being turned into a serpent as ordered by God? You would think that satan would know better after seeing Moses' serpent devour his serpents, which was an outward manifestation of the power of God destroying the works of the devil. Satan knows God's power-his goal is to convince **us** that God's power is the same as his **but** God is Omnipotent and Sovereign!!!

31

I share this with you as a warning today because many are running after a sign and a miracle to please their fleshly desires instead of running after and flowing with the anointing of God. These are dangerous times, know His voice and follow Him, stop running after every wind and doctrine!

...Even him, whose coming is after the working of satan with all power and signs and lying wonders.

II Thessalonians 2:9

It is not the signs and wonders that will get you into glory but the true word and works of God. Moses and the patriarchs of old lived this thing and their works through God were true. You have got to live this! Noah lived this thing called righteousness. Listen to Noah's testimony...

And God saw that the wickedness of man was great in the earth, and that every imagination of the thoughts of man's heart was only evil continually. It is the same today.

Genesis 6:5

And it repented the Lord (it made God's heart sorrowful) that He had made man on the earth. Paraphrased

Genesis 6:6

And the Lord said, I will destroy man who I have created from the face of the earth; both man, and beast, and the creeping thing, and the fowls of the air; for It repenteth Me that I have made them.

Genesis 6:7

If it grieved God's heart for the sins that were in Noah's day, how do you think God's heart feels today with all of the sin and corruption going on in the earth? Do you think that He is pleased with us? I tell you no, He is not pleased. He is grieved!

But Noah found grace **(favor)** in the eyes of the Lord.

Genesis 6:8

Thank God for His grace, and thank God that there are yet some, like Noah, who have the same spirit in our day. Many of you God said, have found that same grace in His eyes. There are yet some just and perfect (mature) men and women of God in our generation. Oh you can go ahead and praise God, He is worthy!

In the days of Noah the same fruit of sin and works of the flesh that we are seeing today were manifested. History has repeated itself, immorality, body piercing, tattooing etc. adultery, fornication, uncleanness, lasciviousness (lustfulness, lewdness, unchasity, wantonness and filth, anything tending to foster sex sin and lust), idolatry, witchcraft, hatred, variance, emulations, wrath, strife, seditions (divisions, parties, popular disorder; stirring up strife in religion, government, home or any other place), heresies, envy, murders, drunkenness, revellings and much the like, all of these things are works of the flesh. If this is your testimony and you are caught up in these things, you need to be saved; you need to be transformed! "All ungodliness is sin". Ask God to save you and bring about a **change** in your life before its too late. God's word warns, they that do these things **"shall not"** inherit the Kingdom of God (Galatians 5:19-21).

*The earth also was corrupt before God, and the earth was (filled) with violence, and **God looked upon the earth** and behold, it was corrupt for all flesh had corrupted their way upon the earth.* It is the same today.

Genesis 6:11-12

*And God said unto Noah, the end of all **flesh** is come before Me, for the earth is filled with violence through them; and behold, I will destroy them with the earth.* God pronounced His judgment and wrath.

Genesis 6: 13

This behavior, conduct and character brought God's severe judgments, ending the dispensation of conscience at that time, just as His judgments and wrath will end the dispensation of grace at His second coming. **WAKE UP and LISTEN**, "Thus saith the Lord tell My people I am coming soon"!

...For when My judgments are in the earth, the inhabitants will learn righteousness.

Isaiah 26:9

With God's judgments in the land His people will **"learn"** to walk in the way of His judgments; they will learn how to wait for the Lord's leading, desire His name above all names and not blaspheme it. They will remember God and desire Him with their whole heart, mind and **body**, and will seek Him early. The inhabitants (the people) will **learn** righteousness by chastening, the wicked will **learn** and recognize God in all His grace, mercy and dealings with them. The saved and the unsaved have lessons to learn.

The Testing of Travail

When God spoke reproof to the churches in the book of Revelation, there were a few that He was somewhat against. So it is with us today! God reveals, "as a woman having birth pains going through travail, testing, and sufferings, so have we been tried, tested, and chastened and we have not birthed souls into the Kingdom according to His will.

We have not caused the kind of deliverance in the earth that He is expecting and the world cannot do it. Even in all of our pain and sufferings we have produced little "saith the Lord". He is somewhat against us!

We have not subdued or converted the Gentile nations. God said, "we have as it were brought forth wind," therefore, the inhabitants of the world cannot come forth. Many were in labour and in pain but gave birth to nothing.

Remember, you have been saved so that the life of Jesus can be seen in you. What ever the trial demands of you go through for righteousness sake and the sake of souls. Like Stephen, yield your body and soul to God.

As saints of God, we have done a lot of false advertising. I often tell Christians, if your testimony of being saved, sanctified, Holy Ghost filled and fire baptized, is not demonstrated in your life, if people do not see Christ's character manifested in you, you may as well take your signs down because its false advertisement. You can testify of this until Jesus comes but if you don't live it, it profits you nothing. Many have been as the word describes in *Psalm 1:1* standing in the way of sinners... having a **form** of godliness. We need to live the life that we testify of and be real!

We have been bound by traditions too long. God declared in His word "the traditions of the elders have made His word ineffective and this is why so many of God's people in the church is going through. God said "many have been doing the work of God but not the will of God." It is His will that pleases Him and His will that produces. Proof producers in the body of Christ must come forth. It is time for a **change,** and it is God that's bringing the change.

Prophetically speaking, the continual travail and testing that is coming will produce a change in us, a change for righteous living. Change is inevitable and if we are going to have an effect on this world for Jesus Christ, **we** must change!

It is now revealed that everyone is going through the *tests of travail*. All creation is waiting for the glorious revelation of the sons of God. The creation is waiting to see Christ in us.

Until this present time, we know that the whole created universe groans in all its parts as if in pains of childbirth. Paraphrased

Romans 8:22

We are all going through trying **(testing)** times, difficult times, turbulent times and evil times. **NOW!**

"All things come alike to all" ...
Ecclesiastes 9:2

God revealed in His word through Hezekiah... "This is a day of trouble and of rebuke, and of blasphemy, for the children are ready for birth and there is not strength to bring forth (Isaiah 37:3) Paraphrased.

As in the days of Hezekiah, so it is in these times and even worse. The body of Christ must travail in prayer and intercession to give birth to souls that are destined to be saved and to come into the Kingdom. We must be a living example of faith, love, mercy, compassion and righteousness. We must live a holy lifestyle; showing forth God's character.

The Apostle Paul's message to the Galatians were; "my little children, of whom **I travail in birth again until Christ be formed in you** *(Galatians 4:19)*. Paul desired to see spiritual restoration, spiritual birth and spiritual growth.

Many of God's people today just want an emotional and spiritual fix, they just want to feel good. **"No pain, no gain"**. People of God giving birth hurts! It's not all about how you feel; it's all about God's souls and His love for them. It does not matter how much the pains hurt as long as it gives Christ an opportunity to be manifested and glorified through you, whom He purchased with His own blood. Paul's thorn in the flesh was painful, it was hurtful but God revealed, "My grace is sufficient Paul! For My strength is made perfect in weakness". Paul resided in the fact that he would rather glory in his infirmities that the power of Christ may rest upon his life.

*Therefore, I take pleasure in infirmities, in reproaches, in necessities, in persecution, in distresses for Christ's sake: for when I am weak, **then** am I strong.*

II Corinthians 12:10

Consider this, are you willing to go through travailing hurting, suffering, testing or whatever it takes for someone to be born into the Kingdom? Are you willing to go through for the sake of souls; are you willing to go through for Christ's sake? Do you remember that Christ was a suffering Servant for you?

Watch this... *"Blessed be the God and Father of our Lord Jesus Christ, the Father of mercies and God of all comfort; who comforts us in all our tribulation **(testing)**, that we may be able to comfort them which are in any trouble, by the comfort wherewith we ourselves are comforted by God."*

II Corinthians 1:3-4

People of God we go through our suffering and testing to be able to comfort others. You are going through and learning a lesson in suffering and God is allowing it so that you will be able to comfort others in their going through.

37

There is a Holy Spirit school of compassion, which consists of **tested saints** who have suffered great things for the Gospel's sake. How can you have compassion on others if you have never gone through anything? You must trust God in your sufferings and submit to whatever test, whatever task He allows to teach you in this Christian walk. He will heal you! He is faithful.

When a woman is pregnant with child the travail comes, severe pain is manifested first, and then a breakthrough, "the soul is birthed" then the healing comes. I am a mother of three God given children and I can boldly tell you "it hurts, child bearing hurts, travail hurts, giving birth **will hurt** but we must suffer through it, as many of us do.

If we are going to birth souls into the kingdom, remember, after the suffering then the blessing (the baby, the soul, the seed), what a joy, what a blessing, what a healing! It is even a greater blessing knowing that "The fruit of the womb is His reward. He is the one that gives the natural and the spiritual birth.

Lo, children are a heritage of the Lord: and the fruit of the womb is His reward.

Psalm 127:3

Paul had a great ministry of travail (suffering). He was anointed for such (Acts 9:16) and so are many of you. God will reveal to you and use you in such a ministry of testing and travail, because you too are a chosen vessel, a chosen instrument for His glory. You too must go through many things and suffer great things for His name's sake. Christ speaks of a fellowship of His sufferings, which is a fellowship of **shared** sufferings. If you are going to reign with Him, you too are going to have to walk through this thing.

I know that many theologians say that we do not suffer for Christ sake but the word confirms that we must suffer.

That I may know Him, and the power of His resurrection, and the fellowship of His sufferings, being made conformable unto His death.
Phillipians 3:10

I encourage you today with the word of God... And this is a faithful saying, "If we *endure* the suffering or whatever we go through for His name sake, we shall reign with Him," Christ gives us reigning power.

So rejoice in knowing that from your suffering and going through, no matter what the task or **test** that you will receive reigning power here and now. God has called us not only to a heavenly reign but also an earthly reign with Him, as His word reveals, we are already seated in heavenly places in Christ Jesus.

Listen to the prophet Isaiah's account of travail, suffering and testing...

*For it is a day of (a time of) **trouble** and **treading down**, and of perplexity by the **Lord God of host** in the valley of vision, breaking down the walls and crying to the mountains.*

Isaiah 22:5

Notice that the word stated, **"by the Lord God of Host"**, not the devil, but "the Lord God of Host"! We are experiencing a time of crushing trouble, confusion and disaster all around us. **It is a day of panic and terror from the Lord, a day of adversity**. God has to bring about such a day or no flesh will be saved. The judgment and wrath of God will produce repentance from sin, causing salvation and bringing healing and deliverance in His people and our land. We will **learn** to obey.

If My people, which are called by My name, shall humble themselves, and pray, and seek My face, and turn from their wicked ways: then will I hear from heaven, and will forgive their sins, and will heal their land.

II Chronicles 7:14

God is speaking to the heart and ears of His people, the saved with wicked ways, but also the wicked unsaved. If we repent and turn, God is faithful to forgive and heal but if not, judgment and wrath will produce repentance.

We learn through **adversity**, a tool used to grow us up, to produce maturity, to produce righteousness, to propel us to the next level in Christ. We should pray that we not murmur and complain when adversity comes; instead of murmuring and complaining we should question "what am I to **learn** in this **test**, God what is your purpose for me in this **test**? Remember, it is a test, pass it!

During these times of trouble, trouble, trouble, our God has already warned us that affliction does not come from the dust, nor does trouble spring from the ground; **yet man is born to trouble as the sparks fly upward**. Trouble will come but we also have a way of escape. God has made a way for us to escape.

The word of the Lord, which came to Zephaniah, is now revealed unto the prophets of our day…the great day of the Lord is near; it is near and hastens quickly. The noise of **the day of the Lord is bitter** (a day of bitter crying out), a day of wrath, terror, trouble, distress, disaster, agony, and a day of the trumpet and alarm **(warning)**. Paraphrased.

God said this day of tribulation **(testing)** must come because of man's sins and trespasses against the Lord.

Heed the warnings; judgment has already begun, even at the house of the Lord, it's in many of our churches where God said it would first begin.

As we the people of God witness this day, we see where immorality is commonly accepted and viewed as normal. We are in the days when man is calling good evil and evil good, calling wrong right and right wrong. Man will not endure sound doctrine but after their own lusts they are running about to hear and follow those who proclaim new ideas of their own inventions, to themselves as teachers, having itching ears; and they are turning away from God's truth and listening to lies. Truly this will evoke God's woes upon mankind, testing of sore travail, His judgments and wrath.

God's judgments are in the earth, heed the warnings as the prophet Isaiah has warned, ..."For when Your judgments are in the earth, the people will **learn** righteousness."

...For when Thy judgments are in the earth, the inhabitants of the world will learn righteousness.
Isaiah 26:9

Lord, when Thy hand is lifted up, they will not see: but they shall see, and be ashamed for their envy at the people; the fire of Thy enemies shall devour them.

Isaiah 26:11

With God's hand lifted up in judgment, we will learn how to live by God's standards of right living, holy living and not our fleshly lustful desires. Again I say unto you, *we have a lesson to learn! God's judgments are in the land hear and believe His word!*

Chapter III

BELIEVE THE REPORT

It is **testing** time! In the book of Isaiah the prophet emphatically asks... **Who has believed our report?** In other words, who has seen the Lord's hand in this, who has **believed**, trusted in, relied upon and clung to our message of that which was **revealed to us**?

Who has believed our report? And to whom is the arm of the Lord revealed?

Isaiah 53:1

I exhort you today to believe the report, for this is a season of diverse testing. Prophets are sent even in our day to warn God's people and to prepare them, not to scare them.

Let me share a few **keys** with you, a few reports, I invite you to get your Bible and flow with me in the anointing through biblical truths.

Jeremiah's Report: When Jeremiah the prophet was sent to **warn Judah** of their captivity because they had kindled a fire in God's anger by their sins; this was God's word to them. "You will be like a barren bush in the desert and you will not enjoy the **seasons of change**". This was a judgment message to His people, and do you think that we will escape God's judgments in our day when many are guilty of the same acts?

*The **sin** of Judah is written with a pen of iron, and with the point of a diamond: it is graven upon the table of their heart, and upon the horns of your altar; **while their children remember** their altars and their groves by the green trees upon the high hills.*

Jeremiah 17:1-2

O My mountain in the field, I will give your substance and all your treasures to the spoil, and your high places for sin, throughout all your borders.

Jeremiah 17:3

God hates sin and He warned His people that they would not continue in the heritage He had given them; He told them He would cause them to serve their enemies in a land, which they knew not of. Judgment?

... "For "you have kindled a fire in My anger, which shall burn for ever.

Jeremiah 17:4

These were God's words to His people. Today we try to eradicate the truth by saying, "a loving God would not do this or allow this to come upon His people" He is reminding us today that He will!

"Now these things were our examples, to the intent we should not lust after evil things as they also lusted".

I Corinthians 10:6

These things were written as examples. God pronounced this **test** of judgment because of their evil practices; their hearts had departed from the Lord. They had gone into captivity because of their wickedness and sins. God knows all of our hearts and there is a penalty for sin. Judgment!

*The heart is deceitful above all things, and **desperately** wicked: who can know it?*

Jeremiah 17:9

I the Lord search the heart, I try (test) the reins, even to give every man according to his ways, and according to the fruit of his doings.

Jeremiah 17: 10

"The test will come to manifest **hidden sins** in our hearts and lives and to produce righteous living and righteous fruit. When we sow seeds of disobedience and wickedness, we cause ourselves to go into captivity and we reap God's judgment and wrath upon us.

*The wrath of God is revealed from heaven **against all** ungodliness and unrighteousness of men, who hold the truth in unrighteousness...*

Romans 1:18

Because that which may be known of God is manifest in them, for God has showed it unto them.

Romans 1:19

God knows our heart, He sees our wrong doings and He has already showed us what is right and what is wrong. His people know the truth but fail to obey Him. We will be judged if we don't repent and turn. "The heart is deceitful above all *things*, and **desperately** wicked as He has stated, who can know it"? God does! It is time to cry out to God for deliverance. When we cry out for deliverance and turn, God is faithful to forgive us and heal us, for our healing and salvation is of God. Have you not heard how David when he was in distress cried unto the Lord **many times** and He heard and delivered him?

*Heal me, O Lord, and I shall be healed; **save me** and I shall be saved, for Thou art my praise.*

Jeremiah 17:14

Jeremiah was commanded by God to go down to the potter's house. God said, "I want to talk with you there, I have something to show you Jeremiah". As Jeremiah watched God manifest a revelation on the potter's wheel, He showed him that the vessel that He made was **marred** (blemished) in His hands. So God made the vessel over again as it seemed good to Him to make. Then God spoke of His people saying...

O house of Israel (My people), cannot I do with you as this potter? saith the Lord. Behold, as the clay is in the potter's hand, so are you in My hand, O house of Israel.

Jeremiah 18:6

*At what time I shall speak concerning a nation (people), and concerning a kingdom, to pluck up, and to pull down, **and to destroy it**; If that nation, against whom I pronounced (judgment) turn from their evil, I will repent of the evil that I thought to do unto them.*
Jeremiah 18:7-8

*Now therefore, go and speak to the men of Judah, and to the **inhabitants** of Jerusalem, saying, Thus saith the Lord; behold, **I frame evil against you**, and devise a device against you: **return** you now everyone from your evil way, and make your ways and your doings good.*
Jeremiah 18:11

This was God's threatening of judgment against His people because of their sins. God hates sin! So when you are so quick to say that God will not bring judgment against His people, my question to you is, **"do you know Him"**?

45

When God threatened in the book of Leviticus Chapter 26, read the account, especially the **key** in verse **15**... "I also will do this unto you when you hate My judgments and statues, when you will not obey and do all of My commandments and if you break My covenant" (paraphrased). God is saying this is what I will do unto you...

"I also will do this unto you; I will even appoint over you **terror***,* **consumption***, and the burning ague, that shall consume the eyes,* **and cause sorrow of heart***: and you shall sow your seed in vain, for* **your enemies shall eat it***.*

Leviticus 26:16

And if you will not yet for all this hearken unto Me, then I will punish you seven times more for your sins.

Leviticus 26:18

Believe the report - it is still God's word today. God said to Judah, His people...

"Behold, I will set My face **against you** *for evil, and to cut off all Judah.*
Jeremiah 44:11

God said, "*I do it*"!

The Omnipotent God reveals, *"I form the light, and create darkness: I make peace, and* **create evil***:* **I the Lord do all these things** *".*
Isaiah 45:7

Know that God means what He says and says what He means. He is a Man of His Word! His Word is sure. God's word is settled and who can change it?

46

God is moving throughout the world, and His judgments are revealed. Heed His Word **today**!

Ezekiel's Report: God's mandate to Ezekiel was to cry, howl, and warn His people that judgment was coming upon them... "For it shall be upon **My people**, it shall be upon all the princes of Israel: **it is destined for My people**, **terror** by reason of the sword **(judgment)** shall be upon **My people**: smite therefore upon thy thigh because it is a **trial**, it is **a test** "saith the Lord God".

Cry and howl, son of man: for it shall be upon My people, it shall be upon all the princes of Israel: terrors by reason of the sword shall be upon My people: smite therefore upon thy thigh.

Ezekiel 21:12

Because it is a trial, (test) and what if the sword contemn even the rod? It shall be no more, saith the Lord God.

Ezekiel 21:13

As God gave Ezekiel this warning to give His people, He is giving us as prophets and leaders today the same warning. God said, "I am **testing** My people, and if they refuse to repent, all these things will come upon them". The Ezekiel's of our day can stand in the gap and make up the hedge. We can give God's people the truth and intercede for them that God gives them a heart to repent and turn at the preaching of the gospel, that when judgment comes they will be under His covering. Pastors, ministers and leaders in the body of Christ, God is sending this warning **especially to us**.

We must get right and lead His people in the right direction, we must be an example. We are not exempt from God's judgments! When we as leaders turn and sin as the world does and do not give God's people the truth and live the example thereof, we bring God's woes, judgment and wrath upon us. "The wrath of God comes upon the children the (people) of God that do not listen and obey Him. God said to His prophet, and is saying to His leaders and ministers, "when a **righteous** man (the saved) turns from his righteousness, and commits sin, and I lay a stumbling block before him, he shall die"; **because you did not warn him**, he shall die in his sin, and his righteousness shall not be remembered. Judgment?

...But his blood will I require at your hand. Nevertheless, if you warn the **righteous** that the righteous sin not, **(if he repent and turn)**, he shall live because of the warning and you have delivered the soul. (Paraphrased)

Ezekiel 3:20-21

God's woes are already upon the disobedient pastors and leaders that have destroyed and scattered His people (His sheep). They have driven them away and have not taken care of them as He commanded. Many have been wounded, used, abused, accused, offended and not fed spiritually or physically. God's people are hurting, and He said, "you have not visited them to heal their hurts". Their needs have not been met and God is holding pastors responsible and accountable.

Woe be unto the pastors that destroy and scatter the sheep of My pasture! Saith the Lord.
Jeremiah 23:1

48

Therefore thus saith the Lord God of Israel against the pastors that feed My people; you have scattered My flock, and driven them away, and have not visited them: behold, I will visit upon you the evil of your doings, saith the Lord.

Jeremiah 23:2

Because of this it has caused God to visit His house. Judgment has come to the **"House"** as stated in Peter...

For the time is come that judgment must begin at the house of God: and if it first began at us, what shall the end be of them that obey not the gospel of God?
I Peter 4:17

God is moving **"in the house"** now, His house, and He reveals that His **ministers** are profane and not tending to the sheep. This is why judgment will begin first in the churches and it's happening. **"It's testing time!"**

For both prophet and priest are profane; yes, in My house have I found their wickedness, saith the Lord.

Jeremiah 23:11

An encouraging word is that we are in the days when God is setting up **shepherds** after His own heart that will feed His flock, heal their wounds and hurts, and tend to their needs. God said, "**I will set up shepherds** over them which shall feed them; and they shall fear no more, nor be dismayed, **neither shall they be lacking**, saith the Lord". (Paraphrased).

And I will gather My flock out of all countries where I have driven them, and will bring them again to their folds; and they shall be fruitful and increase.

Jeremiah 23:3

49

Believe The Report

And I will set up shepherds over them, which shall feed them: and they shall fear no more, nor be dismayed, neither shall they be lacking, saith the Lord.

Jeremiah 23:4

God said in *Revelation 3:10,* **tribulation** (hardship) has come upon **all,** and He means **ALL**! All are being tried and tested, saint and sinner alike, **all** are going through something, one hardship or another in these times. No one will escape God's test, it is a time of great sifting. God said, "it is My time now"! All that's left is time to live for Jesus.

God is moving speedily today, and in His awesome move and revealing we will know the holy from the profane, the real from the unreal in Christ. We will really know who is living for Jesus. It's time to make a difference in the church and in the world. We need to affect the world for Jesus. Jeremiah's inquiry is still, who will believe our report? **Believe the report!**

The report of John The Baptist: There was a man sent from God whose name was John. When asked, who are you, that we may give an answer to those who sent us, and what do you say about yourself? John's report was "I am the voice of one crying in the wilderness: **make straight the way of the Lord,** as the prophet Isaiah said." That voice is still forewarning us today, to "make straight His way" (do it God's way by His methods). God's word is the way and His word will show you the way. "This is the believer's walk of victory".

The report of the ten virgins: Jesus is coming soon, be ready! The report of the ten virgins admonishes us to have our lamps filled with oil, as Jesus is coming looking for His light **in** us! We must have the **oil** of the anointing (the Holy Spirit) to generate the light or we will be unprepared when the Bridegroom comes. You will not have time to share or shop.

Listen to the report of the five wise to the five foolish, when the foolish reported that they had no oil because their lamps had gone out, and requested of the wise to share their oil. The wise answered, saying not so; "we will not give up our oil least there be not enough for us and you, but go to them that sell and buy for yourselves". Look what happened as they were going to shop, while they went to buy. The Bridegroom came and they that were ready went in with Him to the marriage but it was **too late** for the shoppers (they that had lived foolish, unprepared lives) they were left in darkness and missed His coming. "Don't be left behind"!

When the five **unprepared** virgins came knocking on the door, it was **too late**. They said, "Lord open unto us, and He replied, "I don't know you". Don't' let your cry Lord, Lord, be too late, cry out now and be prepared before the door shuts. The word of God warns us in Matthew to **"WATCH"**! The servant is warning us to watch and be prepared. Be ready, for you do not know the day or hour that Jesus is coming. Believe the report and live it, and you shall surely be prepared. God's word is your report!

Watch therefore, for you know neither the day nor the hour wherein the Son of man cometh.

Matthew 25:13

Hear the report of the sower; when anyone hears the word of God and does not understand the word, satan comes and snatches it away from his heart and robs him of the word that has been sown in his mind. This happens to those who receive the word by the wayside, passively.

Now he who receives the seed (the word) among thorns is he who hears the word but lets the cares and desires of this life (the world), and deceitfulness of riches choke the message, and therefore, stops the growth process of the word in him and that individual has no fruit of righteousness.

51

But he who receives the seed (the word) on rocky places, hears the word and immediately receives it with joy and it takes no real root in him, this person, when suffering tribulation *(testing)* or persecution come, because of the word he at once gives up, stumbles and falls. He is **offended by the word and insulted**. We see that this is quite evident even in our day!

They on the rock are they, which, when they hear, receive the word with joy; and these have no root, which for a while believe, and in time of temptation fall away.

Luke 8:13

He who receives the seed (the word) on good ground, is the one who continues to hear and understand the word, bears and produces; some hundred, some sixty, and some thirty times as much as was sown. Receive the word and believe the gospel! God is looking for fruit bearers, fruit producers as revealed in His word.

But the fruit of the Spirit is love, joy, peace, longsuffering, gentleness, and goodness, faith, meekness, temperance: against such there is no law.

Galatians 5:22-23

Don't allow your **testing** to cause you to fall away from God. The emotional hearers, the passive believers in the Parable of The Sower heard the word and like many today, shouted all over the word, got excited, had a good feeling, stayed with God for a while yet did not allow the word to take a deep root in them, so when the testing came they turned away from God and did not stand or pass the test.

I will keep you, "saith the Lord", because you have kept My word patiently, you have walked in My word, and obeyed Me".

It is written, that tribulation **(testing)** worketh patience and this is the reason you are forewarned, you have need of patience, that you might be able to endure in the time of tribulation and testing. There is an experience connected to every test and that experience will help you pass the test in times to come because you know that if He brought you through one trying situation and trauma, He will bring you through anything. The glory in tribulation is knowing that God will bring you through anything. God can! God will!

But we glory in tribulations also; knowing that tribulation worketh patience; and patience, experience; and experience, hope: and hope maketh not ashamed; because the love of God is shed abroad in our hearts by the Holy Ghost which is given unto us.

Romans 5:3-4

If we **live by God's Spirit** our walk will show evidence of Christlike characteristics, and if we are producing His fruit, someone is going to see it and be affected by it. Christ in us is the world's example!

John the Revelator's report: The revelation of Jesus Christ, which God gave unto him, to show unto His servants things which must shortly come to pass; and He sent and revealed it by His angel unto his servant John.

*"I John, who also am your brother, and **companion in tribulation (testing)**, and in the kingdom and patience of Jesus Christ, was in the isle that is called Patmos, for the word of God, and for the testimony of Jesus Christ".*

Revelation 1:9

John's testimony and witness was "I was in the Spirit on the Lord's Day and heard behind me a great voice, as of a trumpet **(warning)**, saying, I am Alpha and Omega, the first and

53

the last; and **what you see, write in a book and send it unto the seven churches.** God's word to John was, **"warn the church, My people, of what is soon to befall them"**.

"He who has an ear let him **hear** what the Spirit says to the churches," travail through all of your testing. **Believe the report.**

Write the things, which you have seen, and the things which are, and the things, which shall be hereafter...

Revelation 1: 19

God is warning and sending the same word to the churches today. We are His church, we are His tabernacles, and we are His building! God has revealed many things about His church and we must **warn** as John warned in his day. Read God's word and **believe** the report!

In this time of testing, endure! You can through Christ. It is written, because you have kept My command to **persevere** Jesus encourages, "I will keep you from **"the hour of trial" (the hour of testing) which shall come upon the whole world, to test those who dwell on the earth**... "Behold, I come **quickly** saith the Lord", hold fast **(hold on)** to what you have, let no one take your crown (your reward).

Remember, "saith the Lord", I taught you how to pray in the time of trouble and distress, in the time of tribulation and testing that you do not enter into temptation. I knew that these times would come and I forewarned you, that you be not put through the **test** as the world. I warned you to watch and pray that you enter not into temptation by disobedience.

Faith On Trial By Fire

Wherein you greatly rejoice, though now for a season, if need be, you are in heaviness through manifold temptations:

I Peter 1:6

That the trial of your faith, being much more precious than of gold that perishes, though it be tried (tested) with fire, might be found unto praise and honor and glory at the appearing of Jesus Christ...

I Peter 1:7

And what I say unto you I say unto all, "WATCH"!

Mark 13:37

Jesus is coming soon!

Chapter IV

A REVELATION OF FIRE

Are you building on the right foundation? Are your works pleasing to God? Christ has laid the foundation but we must take heed how we build and what we use to build with... Now if anyone builds on this foundation gold, silver, precious stone, wood, hay, or straw, the day will declare it, (the **character** of each one's work will come to light, the light will show it plainly) because it will be **revealed by fire; the fire will test** each one's work of what sort it is. **The fire will test the quality and worth of every ones work.** Every man's work will be **processed through the fire** to see whether or not it keeps its value. If any man's work shall be burned, he shall suffer loss; but he himself **shall be saved; yet so as by fire (fiery testing), the furnace of afflictions.** When the Lord revealed this prophecy many years ago, I sought Him as to what He meant by, **"the test of fire".** Many of My people are going to go through tribulation, great testing, great afflictions to get the spots and wrinkles out to be made ready to go back with Me when I come, "saith the Lord". There is a price to pay!

The **trial of fire,** a revelation of fire whereby **every man's** works will be tried **(tested)** as God revealed in (I Corinthians 3:13-17).

Do you know that you are the temple of God, and that the Spirit of God dwells in you? Paraphrased

I Corinthians 3:16

There will be a test!

I have overthrown some of you, as God overthrew Sodom and Gomorrah...yet you have not returned unto Me, "saith the Lord".

Amos 4:11

God is speaking the same prophetic word to His people again today; "I have overthrown some of you, as Sodom and Gomorrah"... you have gone through many tests, trials and tribulations **and yet you have not returned unto Me, you have not learned"**.

Peter warns, that by God's great mercy we have been born anew to a living hope through the resurrection to an inheritance **incorruptible and undefiled**, that does not fade away, reserved in heaven for us, who are kept by the power of God through faith for salvation.

Thus saith the Lord, "I have blessed you with My Spirit, gifts, blessings and healings, and it has not caused you to walk in My ways and return unto Me". Now, My blessings and gifting are being replaced by My judgment and wrath. "When My judgments are in the land **then** will the inhabitants **learn** righteousness!"

He further warns, in this you should greatly rejoice, though **now** for a little while, for **a little season if need be, you have been put to grief by various trials, that the testing of your faith**, being much more precious than gold that perishes, **though it be tried, tested with fire**, may be found to praise, honor, and glory, when Jesus Christ appears.

God allows us to know that we have a need to be tested; **the purpose** is that through the **test** many will acknowledge Him, obey Him, praise Him, honor Him in their lifestyle and give Him glory.

David reveals that God does put the righteous to the **test and it is necessary**! Ecclesiastes The Preacher considered that "all things come alike to all, like things happens to the good as well as the bad". God examines all hearts; the fire will try **everyone's** work!

...For the righteous God trieth the hearts and reins.

Psalm 7:9

Again, I remind you of God's word, **"in this world you shall have tribulation",** you will suffer many things, there will be trouble, there will be various **test**, but cheer up, God is with you. Be encouraged at the warnings, all because Jesus loves you. He is not trying to scare you; He is trying to prepare you!

These things I have spoken unto you, that in Me you might have peace. In this world you shall have tribulation; but be of good cheer; I have overcome the world.

John 16:33

Hear Paul's testimony of how he endured **many trials, tribulations, persecutions, afflictions, near death experiences and situations...It's a done deal!** You are already an overcomer through Christ, no matter what you may be going through in this life. Though tribulation, **testing and trials** come, Paul has given testimonies and examples throughout the New Testament, which can encourage you and give you, hope to endure.

"Who shall separate us from the love of Christ? Shall tribulation, distress, or persecution, or famine, or nakedness, peril, or sword"?

Romans 8:35

As it is written, for Thy sake we are killed all the day long; we are accounted as sheep for the slaughter.

Romans 8:36

Nay, in all these things we are more than conquerors through Him that loved us.

Romans 8:37

For I am persuaded, that neither death, nor life, nor angels, nor principalities, nor powers, nor things present, nor things to come, nor height, nor depth, nor any other creature, shall be able to separate me from the love of God, which is in Christ Jesus our Lord. **Nothing!**

Romans 8:38-39

No matter what you are going through, you must be fully persuaded that you are more than a conqueror because Jesus loves you! The Holy Spirit sheds his love abroad in your heart and **His love will endure anything, love bears all things**. Paul was fully **persuaded**, that nothing could ever separate him from God's love, **not even sufferings, tribulation or death**. He knew and was persuaded in whom he believed. Paul endured many **trial by fire tests**. God proved him and he proved faithful.

We learn that truth remains, even in our sufferings. Through our suffering we also **learn** obedience, love and devotion and that we must be **willing** to obey even beyond the suffering. The word of God reveals that Jesus through His suffering **learned** obedience and since He Himself has been through suffering, **testing and temptations**, He knows what it's like when we suffer and are tempted. He is wonderfully able to comfort, help and deliver.

We must go through our suffering and obedience to God so that **others** can be saved, delivered and made free. "He came to set the captive free, this was His purpose and it is our purpose also. God uses our **tests** and experiences to help others through their tests and experiences. **It's all about His souls!**

I remember some years ago when I was ministering in Roxboro, North Carolina in an open-air service to a group of people, God prophesied and these were His words, "I know Mine, I have not lost a one, and I will bring My people if I have to bring them blind, maimed, cripple or crazy". I feared and I literally shook at those words. God revealed that He loves his own, He died for us and He will not lose a one of us. I realized that before He does, he will bring us by **any means necessary**, that's how much He loves us.

Through the crucible of afflictions many will have to come, in order to get prepared to go back with Christ when He comes. "As He proclaims none but the righteous shall see God". There must be a cleansing process for Christ to present us a glorious church, not having spot, winkle, or blemish. We must be holy and without blame, our garments must be pure white. The heat of the fire of **testing** will purify and rid God's people of winkles, spots and blemishes.

Remember Sampson, God's man once highly anointed and how his disobedience to God cost him his hair, strength, eyes, life and anointing? Like Sampson, many of My people are going to go through tribulation, **fiery testing**, great afflictions to get the spots and wrinkles out, "saith the Lord". There is a price to pay! Sampson paid a terrible price for his sin; **through the crucible of afflictions** God saved him as **by fire.**

If any man's work shall be burned, he shall **suffer loss: but he himself shall be saved, "yet as by fire".** The fire of afflictions will get the work done. **There has to be a spiritual refining.**

60

Sampson had to go through a refining process to enter in to the Kingdom of Heaven and even though he lost much, he did not lose his salvation.

I have ministered to many in hospitals, mental institutions, nursing homes, prisons, jails, street ministry, jobs, etc., and it saddens my heart to see those who once knew God and would not retain Him in their knowledge. God has to allow them to go through the process of fiery testing, because they would not listen, to save them. Many walk around with crosses, Bibles, quoting scriptures in one breath and using God's name in vain with the other breath or worse. If you listen to them, they can quote scriptures and tell you what God expects out of you. I thank God for the opportunities to reach them so that God can get their attention and deliver them. Even in the state that many are in, God's mercy and hand is stretched out still. In this day of the Joel prophecy God is pouring out His Spirit upon **all** flesh. We can clearly see that the love and compassion of God is giving His people another chance for righteousness, another chance to hear His word, to turn, become clean and live for Him. God is giving them time to repent and turn to Him. Everyone has an opportunity to seek God and change **now**, getting their lives in order before Him. Our streets are filled with the disobedient and rebellious. **The testing, the trial of fire will produce change in us, purging all, bringing forth righteousness in mankind**.

Many Christians are suffering **"trial by fire"** testing, today, asking, "what's going on, why is this happening, please pray for me"? **It is God's testing to propel you to the next level of glory**. We must change!

*But we all, with open face beholding as in a glass the glory of the Lord, are **changed** into the same image from glory to glory, even as by the Spirit of the Lord.*

II Corinthians 3:18

Watch this! The bible declares, "For unto you it is given in the behalf of Christ, not only to believe on Him, but also to **suffer** (go through whatever test or task) for His name' sake".

Paul reminds us that we will have the same conflicts, which we have seen and heard of him. We are in **spiritual warfare** like never before; our faith is in a fight! Paul had to fight the good fight of faith and he encourages us to do the same. **Go through your testing victoriously without murmuring or complaining and bless Jesus**.

With our faith being **tried by fire**, the depth of our **character** will be revealed. When the fire is turned up seven times hotter, and the pressure seven times greater, this will reveal how we react or hold up under pressure. These tough times, perilous times and difficult times will teach us patience, perseverance and steadfastness. Everyone has to grow up, God is calling us unto maturity now.

Behold, I have refined you, but not with silver; I have chosen you in the furnace of affliction.

Isaiah 48:10

Your afflictions are working for you; what ever you are going through is working for you! It's going to work a more exceeding and eternal weight of glory. It is working together for your good. **Go through!**

God said, "the hour of temptation **(testing)** has come upon the entire world, **all inhabitants,** to try, to **test** them that dwell upon the earth". Testing has come upon saint and sinner alike. There are things that God has to work out of us, and things He has to work in us for His name' sake. So think it not strange concerning the **fiery trial, which** is to **test** you as though some strange thing happened unto you.

Make sure that your attitude is right in the **test producing character change**. Christ admonishes us to rejoice; and have a right attitude inasmuch as we are partakers of His sufferings, because when His glory is revealed, we will rejoice with exceeding joy.

A **time of testing** for the church (God's house, God's people) - For the time is come that **judgment** must begin at the house of God; and if it **first** begins at **us**, what shall the end be of them that do not obey the gospel of God? And if the righteous scarcely be saved, where shall the ungodly and the sinner appear? Wherefore, let them that **suffer according to the will of God commit** the keeping of their souls to Him in well doing, as unto a faithful Creator. "He is faithful, commit and submit!"

We will suffer according to the "will of God"! The scripture said it, "I didn't". So let us go through without murmuring and complaining, for it is when we go through that the Spirit of glory rest upon us. When do we see God's glory? When we go through!

The scripture further admonishes that as Christ has suffered for us in the flesh, we are to arm ourselves likewise with the same mind **(we too must suffer many things)**. His word confirms that if we have suffered in the flesh, we cease from sinning. In other words, our suffering is necessary for obedience, and that we not practice sin. God's plan included suffering...

*For even hereunto were you called: because Christ also suffered for us, leaving us an **example**, that you should follow His steps...*

I Peter 2:21

Again, hear the words of the servant David ... "Before I was **afflicted** I went astray: but **now** have I kept thy word".

Remember, David disobeyed God and it took the affliction to get him back in line with the word of God. David knew God's commandments, he knew God's word! When we go **astray and wander** there is always the Shepherd's rod of chastisement to bring us back in line. David repented and turned and God forgave him.

For you were as sheep going astray, but are now returned unto the Shepherd and Bishop of your souls.

I Peter 2:25

Often times God has spoken and warned us, He has shown us signs that we are out of line with His word and we still don't listen and turn, so He has to speak where it hurts the hardest and then we understand that He is speaking. This shows us that it takes the affliction, it takes the chastisement otherwise, many will not obey and many will be lost.

David testifies of God's goodness and mercy after the affliction, and therefore states, "You are good, and do good, teach me Your statues". He confesses, "**It is good for me that I have been afflicted (punished, chastised); that I might learn Thy statues**".

I know, O Lord, that Thy judgments are right, and that **You in faithfulness have afflicted me**. O hallelujah, hallelujah! This makes my heart rejoice to know that one expresses such honoring of God after a good spanking. David literally praised God for his affliction, his **testing**, and his going through. He knew that it was working together for his good. Read the account in *Psalms 119: 67,68, 71, 75* and let it bless your soul.

It's time to take a praise break! This is a good place to **stop reading** and praise God for your **testing** and the revelation of His word!

Did you think you would not have to suffer anything? Did you think you would just dance and shout your way into heaven without any trials or tribulation, when God has already forewarned that you are going to have them? He warned us through His servant the Apostle Paul that we are to continue in the faith, as **we must** enter the kingdom through **much tribulation**, and many **tests.**

Confirming the souls of the disciples, and exhorting them to continue in the faith, and that we must through much tribulation enter into the kingdom of God.

Acts 14:22

Paul sent Timothy a brother and minister of God, to comfort God's people concerning their faith in suffering and afflictions that they be not moved by them. He also warned them that we are appointed unto afflictions and tribulation, **tests** of many kinds. This was their report to the Thessalonians...

"For verily when we were with you, we told you before that we should **suffer tribulation**, even as it came to pass, and you know".

I Thessalonians 3:4

God knows our tribulation and He will not allow anymore to be put on us than we can bear. Praise God!

Through the crucible of fiery trials of national disasters, persecution, affliction and suffering, we will learn the lesson of obedience and submission to God. As we see national disasters unfolding all over the world through, storms, earthquakes, winds, fires, etc., it is a manifestation of God's judgments. God is moving throughout the earth and He is having His way.

A Revelation Of Fire

God revealed that He has His way in the whirlwinds, tornados and storms. He also revealed that He is slow to anger and in great power, and will not at all acquit the wicked.

...The Lord has His way in the whirlwind and in the storm and the clouds are the dust of His feet.

Nahum 1:3

Let me take a moment and encourage you with a revelation of glory here! Did you know that when you look up and see the clouds you are looking at God's glory? They are the evidence that God is moving, for the clouds Nahum declare, are the dust of His feet.

It is time to stop and give God a praise offering!

God Is The One Proving Us!

In this time of tribulation meaning, **trial, affliction**, hardship, cross, **crucible**, ordeal, and visitation, we are being **tested, proven, and approved**. God is putting us to the **test**. He is the one writing the testing.

Remember in the Old Testament when the people were afraid of God's presence after witnessing the thundering and lightning flashes, the sound of the trumpet and the mountain smoking; when they saw it, they trembled and stood afar off. Then they said to Moses, "you speak with us, and we will hear; but let not God speak with us, least we die."

And Moses said to the people, "Do not fear; for God has come to prove you, that His fear may be before your faces, that you sin not."

Exodus 20:20

"God **proved them, He tested** His people to see if they would reverence and obey Him. **God will allow trials in our lives in order to test our devotion and love to Him**.

Moses also put them in remembrance of God's commandments to be careful and observe them. He reminded them how God had led them through the wilderness for forty years to **humble and test them**, to know what was in their heart, and to know if they would keep His word.

Today we are being warned and **tested for the same purpose**, to teach us and to see if we will humbly obey God's word and reverence Him, to see if we will obey His voice the written and spoken word.

God's prophets are carrying the same message of repentance and warnings today. Heed the warning, listen to the prophets and don't take their message lightly, before sudden destruction comes upon you. **Fiery testing is here**! **The refiner's fire is here**! God is bringing us through the refining process. **Judgment is in the land, please take heed!**

CHAPTER V

WHEN GOD PERMITS THE TEST

What Happens When The Test Is "Throw Jonah Overboard?"

Like the Prophet Jonah, many today are running in the opposite direction of where God is sending or leading them. When this happens it will always bring one into difficult times and troubled waters, especially for failure to obey God's command.

God is **testing** our obedience to His word in this hour. We are living in the last days and the revelation of God warns that **"testing" shall come upon all"** as shared earlier. **All are being tested** saint and sinner alike. Things are happening in our lives to show us that God is serious about His word to us. When He gives a command, He expects it to be carried out just as ordered. Like Jonah, we must learn that God's concerns are about obedience and love for His souls.

God spoke to Jonah and commanded him to go to Nineveh and cry out against that great city and **warn** them of their wickedness and sins, which had come up before Him. Does this remind you of the people of our world today? There is so much wickedness and sin and God is sending warnings before His punishment of judgment and wrath begin to fall. Are we hearing? Are we crying out?

God had one plan and focus in mind souls, but Jonah had his own agenda. One should never disobey an assignment ordered by God. When we do, know that we are headed for a fiery trial. Jonah's obedience and love was tested. He failed the test.

68

Jonah tried to flee and hide from God's presence but found himself in the belly of a giant fish created by the very One he was running from. Through this fiery trial Jonah learned about the mercies of God. In the fiery trial Jonah learned that what God says He means. God's purpose will be accomplished! He learned that what God speaks, God will bring to pass. Jonah learned to obey.

*So shall My word be that goeth forth out of My mouth: it shall not return to Me void, but it shall accomplish that which I please, and it shall **prosper** in the thing whereto I sent it.*
Isaiah 55:11

God is concerned and cares about all people. When one chooses to disobey and not give them His warnings, one causes God's anger to be kindled. I know that when testing and adversity comes it is often said that it's the devil, the devil, the devil, we fail to realize that God is Sovereign. It is not always the devil on our case; God has a purpose to accomplish!

Watch this! Many today say, "that's not God, the loving God would not allow one of His to be thrown into the sea and swallowed by a giant fish, God would not allow disaster to come upon His people." Don't tempt God, read His word! From Genesis to Revelation since the fall of Adam, God has shown examples of trouble, adversity, captivity, wars and disaster upon His people because of sin and disobedience. There is a price to pay for disobedience which is sin!

Many often fail to realize that there is a penalty for sin, there are consequences. Jonah went through much tribulation, testing, adversity and trouble because of his sin of disobedience.

We need to remember that when we repent and turn, God's mercy always prevails. Look at His mercy extended to Jonah - God prepared a giant fish for his protection and deliverance in spite of his disobedience. God knew Jonah's heart. He knew that Jonah would repent, and He also knew that it would take **adversity** to bring him to repentance. This is a great example of truth to observe; when we sin we have an Advocate. When we repent and turn, God is faithful to forgive and deliver us. Repent and move on, don't stay in that sinful situation and don't wallow in guilt, as God forgives us, **we must** forgive ourselves.

The Prayer and Cry Of Jonah

Listen to Jonah's prayer and testimony, "I prayed unto the Lord my God out of the fish's belly, and **I cried by reason of my affliction (suffering)** unto the Lord and He heard me; out of the belly of hell, He heard my voice". **Jonah confessed,** "God **You** cast me into the deep, in the middle of the sea; and the floods compassed me about (closed or hedged me in): all **Your** billows and waves passed over me". Jonah then prays a prayer of repentance; I am cast out of **Your** sight; yet I will look again toward Your holy temple. He did not say that the devil did it; **he confessed that God allowed this affliction because of his disobedience.** The waters of affliction compassed me about, even to the soul: the depth closed me round about and weeds were wrapped around my head. I went down to the bottom of the mountains, the earth with her bars was about me forever **(Jonah could see no way out of his dilemma)**: yet You brought up my life from corruption, O Lord my God. Jonah did not eradicate his punishment or his judgment by God as many does today, he confessed that God allowed the afflictions and God brought him up out of them **after repentance.**

70

Remembering God In Trouble

Jonah confessed, **"when my soul fainted within me, I remembered the Lord**: and my prayer came to Him in His holy temple". **Isn't it strange that when adversity comes, when trouble and tribulation come, it has a way of making us remember the Lord?** That tells me something, adversity has its purpose, it is healthy for us spiritually. We are reminded of who God is and His commands. Remember David's testimony in *(Psalms 119:71,75)*. He said, "It is good that I have been afflicted; that I might **learn** thy statues…I know, Lord that Thy judgments are right, and that **Your faithfulness have afflicted me**."

Can you testify of God's goodness for chastising you when you have chosen to rebel and disobey Him? Are you among the ones that say, "God does not chasten His people, God does not bring judgment upon His people"? **Does He really love you that much?** God tells us in His word that those He love, He rebukes and chastens, and if we do not **endure** His chastening we are bastards and not sons.

For whom the Lord love He chastens, and scourgeth every son whom He receives. If you endure chastening, God dealeth with you, as with sons; for what son is he whom the father chasteneth not?

Hebrews 12:6-7

*But if you be without chastisement, **whereof all are partakers**, then are you bastards and not sons.*

Hebrews 12:8

71

David said, "It is good for me that I have been punished, that I have been chastened for my wrong doings!"

Jonah **warns**, if you observe lying vanities you forsake your own mercy. It does not pay to follow your own agenda and disregard your loyalty and obedience to God. Jonah ends his testimony and prayer on this wise - "I will sacrifice unto the Lord with the voice of thanksgiving; I will pay that which I have vowed". Jonah knew to be grateful to God for His goodness and mercy of bringing him out of his disaster and troubles, and he gave a statement of praise, "salvation is of the Lord." He realized that the salvation (deliverance) of this **test** was based upon repenting, obeying, loving and giving thanks to God, and when you make a vow you should pay it.

Now Let's Try It Again Jonah!

Jonah found out that God was the God of another chance. It is good to know that our God does not give up on us easily, hallelujah! God is not slack concerning His promises, when He promises to save, He saves, what He promises to keep, He keeps, when He promises deliverance, He delivers, **"salvation is of the Lord"**! The Bible reveals that the Lord spoke to the fish and it obeyed and vomited out Jonah upon the dry land. Even the fish in the sea obeys God. Do you see the love, mercy, and grace of God in this? God delivers on time. We are victorious.

The word of the Lord came to Jonah the second time, saying, "arise Jonah and go to Nineveh that great city and preach unto it the preaching I tell you".

This time Jonah obeyed, went and preached unto Nineveh and God revealed unto him the love and concern He has for His people, and His mercy upon them when they repent and turn. Jonah had a lesson to learn!

Look at what happens when you obey God; obeying God can turn an entire city around. Jonah obeyed God; the people believed, repented, proclaimed a fast and put on sackcloth, young and old, from the least to the greatest. Nineveh's king acknowledged God in His servant Jonah; the people obeyed God's word repented and were delivered.

What an awakening! The King rose from his throne at the hearing of the word, and published a decree to his nobles saying, let not man, beast, herd or flock, taste anything: let them not feed, or drink water; let man and the animals **cover themselves before God** with sackcloth, and cry mightily unto God, let them **turn** every one from his evil, sinful way and from the violence that they do. Then the King asked a question, "Who can tell if God will turn and repent (change His mind), and turn away from His fierce anger, that we perish not (that He spare our lives)? The loving, merciful God, Creator of mankind saw their works that **they turned** from their evil way; and God repented (changed His mind, and did not inflict on them the **disaster** which He had threatened). Praise our God!

God's Mercy

God is concerned about sparing cities and His people. His nature is not to destroy but if you sin destruction and judgment is already pronounced. However, even in judgment if we repent and turn, His hand is stretched out to deliver us.

Jonah's attitude was not pleasing to God, he was angry with God for changing His mind to spare the city and the people, and it caused him to go through yet another **test**. In his testing, he requested of God to take his life. How selfish of him, this certainly was not God's character. The Lord said to him "are you really angry Jonah"? God prepared a gourd to be a shadow over his head to deliver him from his grief. Jonah was very grateful for the gourd, yet he was not grateful to God for delivering His people. Therefore, God prepared a worm in the morning to attack the gourd and it withered. At the rising of the sun, He prepared a vehement east wind; and the sun beat upon Jonah's head and he fainted and wished to die and said, "it is better for me to die than live". God said to Jonah again "do you have reason to be angry about the gourd"? And Jonah said, "I have good reason to be angry, enough to die". God said to him, you have had mercy on a gourd, which you neither labored or made to grow; which came up in a night, and perished in a night; and should not I have pity on and spare Nineveh, that great city which are more than 120,000 people who cannot discern between their right hand and their left, and also much live stock?

God loves His souls for which He gave His only Begotten Son and does not want one to be lost. Consider the mercy and love He bestowed upon His people in Nineveh.

God's mercy and grace in us should long to see souls saved and delivered no matter what we must go through or what we see them going through. No matter what the **test** or **task**. "His mercy endureth forever"!

The Cup Of Suffering Test

Let me share with you a revelation that the Holy Spirit revealed to me on suffering, persecution and testing ordained of God in Matthew Chapter 20.

A mother came to Jesus requesting and desiring a favor of Him for her two sons. Listen to the remarks of Jesus and the answer to the question asked...

And He said unto her, what is your request? She said unto Him, "grant that these my two sons may sit, the one on Thy right hand, and the other on the left, in Thy kingdom" (Paraphrased).

Matthew 20:21

But Jesus answered, "You don't know what you are asking, are you able to drink of the cup (the suffering and persecution) that I shall drink of, and to be baptized with the baptism that I am baptized with"? They said, "We are able", (we can)! (Paraphrased).

Matthew 20:22

And He said unto them, "You shall drink indeed (you will surely drink) of My cup, and be baptized with the baptism that I am baptized with: but to sit on My right hand, and on My left, is not Mine to give, but it shall be given to them for whom it is prepared of My Father.

Matthew 20:23

These brothers said, **"we are able, we can handle it"**. They had no understanding of what they were asking, and **indeed** suffering and persecution came.

When you go to God with whatever your request, make sure that your motives are pure! The cup of suffering is passed down to every believer. Hear the words of the Lord Jesus "If you suffer with Me, you shall reign with Me"..."Take up your cross saith Jesus and follow Me". Every one that names the name of Christ must carry their cross and the way of the cross is a suffering way, a way of testing, tribulation, persecution and afflictions. Think it not strange!

The Godly In Christ Will Suffer

Consider this, "what if God allows a **test** in your life, what if He chooses to challenge the devil with your obedience, love and faith"? What if God chose to brag on you..."Have you considered My servant _____?" Place your name there. God allowed Job's **test** of afflictions, He allowed his suffering and yet God was there all the time **for** Job. Remember Job was not put through his **test** because of disobedience and sin, but because of his love, obedience and integrity for God.

And the Lord said unto satan, whence comest thou (where did you come from)? Then satan answered the Lord, and said, from going to and fro in the earth, and from walking up and down in it.

Job 1:7

And the Lord said unto satan, have you considered My servant Job, that there is none like him in the earth, a perfect and upright man, one that fears God and hates evil. Paraphrased

Job 1:8

Then satan answered the Lord, and said, does Job fear You for nothing? Paraphrased

Job 1:9

When satan goes to God and accuses you before God of just serving Him for what you can get out of Him and obtains permission to **test you.** When God grants him permission to **test** you, and to **prove** you, will you love God with all your heart still, will you continue to trust and obey Him as Job did? What will happen if God allows the fire to be turned up and the **test** intensifies and you feel like God has forsaken you because you do not understand His purpose? Will you still love and trust Him? You may be going through a **test** now. God will always see you through it and prove satan to be the liar that he is, and you to be the victor that God says you are. The Bible reveals that satan **is** a liar from the beginning; he is the father of lies. You did not forget Adam and Eve's **test** of obedience and how he deceived them in the Garden of Eden, did you?

Don't be disturbed by the trouble and testing you see around you, or the suffering you may be going through right now. God has warned, "don't be soon shaken". You may say, "I love the Lord and trust Him," yet you do not understand why **tests** and **trials** come. Know that God has a **purpose** for every trial and all the suffering you go through. He works it out for your Good. Go through!

Christians suffer trials **(testing)**, tragedies and adversity not necessarily because of sin nor fiery trials because God is angry. As in the wilderness **test** of the Israelites and as seen with Job and many of the patriots of old, God may be testing **(proving)** your faith and love towards Him. Suffering may occur for many reasons that we do not comprehend until or unless God reveals His purpose to us. God was bragging on Job, **proving** Job's integrity and love for Him; He was **testing** him, not punishing him. Job's testimony was not that it was the devil, his testimony was "though God slay me, yet will I trust Him". It's all about trusting God. Job confessed, "all the days of my **appointed time** will I wait, until my **change** come. God has a **perfect timing** set to bring you out of your **test**.

Trials and sufferings provide spiritual enrichment, builds **character and spiritual growth**, and **relationship** between God and us. Remember Jonah? His case was different, he just out right rebelled and disobeyed God. Yet God taught him through his trials.

I love the way the Apostle Paul puts it, if I may paraphrase... Whatever trials, **test**, persecution, disaster, or affliction, whatever I have gone through or must go through, whatever I have lost or will lose, **"I count it all dung (rubbish), that I may know Christ and the power of His resurrection and the fellowship of His sufferings"**. Paul wanted a relationship with God above all other choices. He wanted to know God in reality, in intimacy, in power, spirit and in truth. Paul wanted to please God. **"Know Him"!**

That I may know Him...

Phillipians 3: 10

78

Disaster Touches America

In the midst of this writing, God revealed and confirmed the message He had given to warn His people that their **"faith would be tried by fire"**, and of the **testing** that would come upon them in these times. He also confirmed the prophecy that there would be national disasters and disaster would come to America.

Many have eradicated the judgments and wrath of God for so long, now that it is being manifested, they are in total denial. There are those who do not believe that the loving God would permit or allow such **testing** of disasters and tribulation in the lives of His people, much of it is because of sin, and rebellion before Him. It is a dangerous **misconception** when we eradicate God's judgments and wrath when He has stated that, "the judgments and wrath of God comes upon the children of disobedience" and **testing** comes upon **all"**.

... The hour of temptation (**testing**) *will come upon ALL the world...*

Revelation 3:10

On Tuesday, September 11, 2001, while turning the channels to find a Christian program on television, I saw that a plane had crashed into the World Trade Center in New York. Immediately I turned back to the channel to see what was going on, and as I watched, another plane struck the second tower. Like many Americans, I wondered if this was just another movie. Realizing this was a reality and not a movie, I began to pray for God's mercy and intervention for His people.

It was then God revealed what He had spoken to my heart years ago, that the violent, evil and ungodly movies shown on television was a set up and plan of satan to deceive many of His people, that when real tragedies begin to happen and disasters come, they would not believe. Satan's cunning and deceptive plan is always to deceive God's people away from God and the truth so that they disobey and doubt His word.

Satan wants you to think that the ungodliness you watch on television is just an act, that it's not real! I am here to tell you that the **terror** you watched on television September 11th was very real. I warn you today that more disasters are coming, as the word of God has already warned. He has warned us that man's heart would fail them; there will be heart attacks and deaths because of the things and the **terror** that's coming upon the earth (Luke 21:25-26). It's time for God's people to hear and heed the warnings of God. Learn that He is real, know His word is true and heed His judgments and wrath as being real.

The warning of September 11, 2001 at 8:45 a.m. when American Airlines Flight 11 crashed into the North Tower of the World Trade Center was a **test** that **shook** and is yet **shaking all nations even until this very day**- a wake up call to American and a warning to nations. We are yet facing and will continue to face many **tests**, many trials and much tribulation "saith the Lord". God has warned that everything that can be shaken, will be and is being shaken that those things which cannot be shaken will remain, and unless, your faith is fixed, rooted and grounded in His word and His righteousness, you will be uprooted. It is happening!

Regarding the September 11th tragedy, our President George W. Bush spoke of **"The Test Resolve."** Many since that time, even ministers are yet talking about **"the test"**. Does this make you stop and think of God's warning, **"Faith On Trial By Fire"?** The Lord is preparing us for **Jesus' soon** *coming* and we are being warned of things to come. Many are still saying, "I have been hearing that for years and He didn't come yet". I tell you today, His coming "is a lot closer today than yesterday". This is a true saying and worthy of adhering to. Take heed to this warning!

God has been sending warnings through the years by His preachers, prophets and many other messengers of God that trouble, destruction and **disaster** was coming to America. Many are caught up, not taking heed and are missing the warnings, and there are those that just do not believe as in the days of Noah.

My prayer is that God's servant, President George W. Bush will seek and listen to the voice of God through godly men and women, God's messengers sent to him, calling our country to prayer and repentance before God, as the King did in Nineveh (Jonah 3:7-10), that God might see our repentance, good works, and spare our country and its people.

On September 11th in a day our Twin Towers were destroyed and many lives were destroyed along with it. Within a short period in the same day, our Pentagon in Washington, D.C was struck by disaster and many lives were destroyed. Shortly thereafter, another plane was destroyed in Pennsylvania by **terrorism and disaster** and many lives were destroyed. How much warning and **shaking** do we need to hear of and see, before we look up to God and come before Him with fasting, repentance and turning from our evil deeds and sinful ways in the earth and in our country. God is trying to get His peoples **attention** before it's too late. **Jesus is coming! Jesus is coming! Jesus is coming!** Please take heed.

Let us remember to pray for our government and leaders. In the book of Romans the Apostle Paul admonishes us to be in subjection to magistrates and rulers, **for it is God's ordination.** He admonishes us to **pray** for them because they are God's **ministers** for our good.

Let every soul be subject unto the higher powers. For there is no power but of God: the powers that be are ordained of God.

Romans 13:1

For he is the minister of God to you for good...

Romans 13:4

The Apostle Paul warns God's people to pray and make supplication and intercession for **all,** and in so doing to give thanks to God. Heed this word! "Paul admonishes God's people to pray for kings and **all in authority**". God has a **purpose** in this for His glory and our good, pray ...

For kings, and for all that are in authority; that we may lead a quiet and peaceable life in all godliness and honesty.

I Timothy 2:1-2

For this is good and acceptable in the sight of God our Savior; who will have all men to be saved, and come unto the knowledge of the truth.

I Timothy 2:3-4

We must pray for our precious President and **all** in leadership and in doing so we obey Christ. The reason our country is in a state of chaos, sin and rebellion is because we have not obeyed the commandments of our God to pray and intercede for our leaders, as we should. We need to practice the word spoken in Luke 18:1 **"men ought to always pray"**... We need to pray fervently and earnestly that our government leaders will open the door for prayer and devotion again in our schools, as well as in our government. Prayer is our blessing and covering of protection from God. Prayer and returning to God is the answer to our problems today.

When we rejected God's presence into our schools and government, we left the door open for satan and all of his demons to come in with witchcraft, all ungodliness and perverseness. As a result we have changed our laws, and lowered our standards. We have **abortions,** which is murder, all over our land. We promote condoms in our schools. We promote all kinds of books of satanic learning to our children poisoning and destroying their young minds and hindering their learning ability. Murder and promiscuousness is all over the land. We have angered the heart of our God. **"Ah sinful nation, saith the Lord"!**

Ah sinful nation, a people laden with iniquity (sin), a seed of evildoers, children that are corrupters: they have forsaken the Lord, they have provoked the Holy One of Israel unto anger, they are gone away backward.

Isaiah 1:4

God declares, "when **My judgments** are in the earth, the people of the world will **learn** to do what's right".

The prophet Isaiah testifies, "Lord, **in trouble**, in times of **suffering, affliction, disaster, terror, chastening and testing** have they visited You, they cried out to You, they poured out a prayer when your **chastisement** (punishment) was upon them.

I say to America, the nations, tongues and kindred's **everywhere**, invite Christ into your heart, into your life and invoke His presence and anointing back into your land, your schools and governments. **Repent and turn** back to God that perhaps He will bless and heal our lands, and in the midst of His judgments and wrath He will have mercy.

Hear the word of God concerning His judgments and take heed! "Shall a trumpet be blown in the land, and the people not be afraid? Shall there be evil in a city and the Lord have not done it? Read Amos 3:6. God's hand is stretched out in mercy still. Listen to His warning before it's too late! Listen to His invitation to us...

Come, let us return unto the Lord: for He has torn, and He will heal us; He has smitten, and He will bind us up.

Hosea 6:1

After two days will He revive us: in the third day He will raise us up, and we shall live in His sight.

Hosea 6:2

Then shall we know, if we follow on to know the Lord: His going forth is prepared as the morning; and He shall come unto us as the rain, as the latter and former rain unto the earth.

Hosea 6:3

America, God has torn, He has smitten and He will heal us when we repent and change. So give Him praise!

The Tests and Temptations of Jesus

I purposely saved the **testing example of our Lord Jesus permitted by God** near the ending of this book, to enlighten and encourage you greatly, that His **testing** remains fresh in your minds as we **endure** our hour of temptation revealed in Revelations 3:10.

Because you have kept the word of My patience, I also will keep you from the hour of temptation, which shall come upon all the world, to try (test) them that dwell on the earth. Paraphrased
Revelation 3:10

Thus saith the scriptures, it behoved Jesus to be made like His brethren, that He might be a merciful and faithful High Priest in things pertaining to God, to *make reconciliation for the sins of the people".* For in that **He Himself has suffered being tempted, tested and tried,** He is able to succour them that are **tempted** and **tested.** The **joy** of going through any **test** is knowing that Jesus is with you, (*Emmanuel, God is with us).*

He is there in every test, every trial, in all of your suffering and going through. Now I can understand why James wrote in his book, "Count it **all joy** when you go through **diverse testing".** The **joy** is knowing that God is with you. God is also reminding you that your going **through,** is only for a season, only for a moment. You are not to stay in that season forever!

For in that He himself has suffered being tempted,
He is able to succour them that are tempted.

Hebrews 2: 18

Consider Jesus' test! After the glory of God was manifested upon Jesus at His baptism, and God revealed, **"this is My beloved Son in whom I am well pleased"**... The Bible states "Jesus, being full of the Holy Ghost returned from Jordan and was **led of the Spirit** into the wilderness to be tempted **(tested)** of the devil forty days. And when He had fasted forty nights, He was afterward hungry. The tempter (satan) came to Him, and said, "**if**" you are the Son of God, command that these stones be made bread". **Watch out for satan's "if" challenges!** He tested Jesus at a point of vulnerability, when He was hungry, thirsty and weak. Jesus was tested in His appetite, earthly vision and weakness by the devil. Satan requested of Jesus to fall down before him and worship him. If you are not watchful, full of God's Spirit and His word, satan will tempt you to fall down and worship him also. Jesus passed the test! You can too!

But Jesus answered and said, ..."*It is written, that man shall not live by bread alone, but by every word of God*".

Luke 4:4

...Thou shall not **test** the Lord your God. Paraphrased

Luke 4:12

If you are going to have victories in every **test**, you too must speak the word of God. **Learn** a lesson from Jesus our Savior and **pass the test!** There is power in the Word to defeat every snare, every trick, and every test of the devil. **Resist** the devil and he will flee.

There were other **tests** that satan tempted Him with but Jesus resisted. Read the story in Luke 4:1-13. He was also tempted, tested and accused by religious leaders, churchgoers.

What if the Holy Spirit led you into your **wilderness experience** to be **tested** by the devil? Would you remain faithful and use the weapons already available to you through Christ, the word of God, or would you just murmur and complain with a woe is me spirit? Many do not want to go through **testing** for one day, let alone forty days. **Think about it!**

Often times our testimony is "I don't know why God let this happen to me or Lord what have I done now, why am I going through this"? It comes against all of us at one time or another. God's answer to you is, "In this world you will have tribulation (trouble)." This is why you are going through! You are going through because you are in a real **warfare**. Paul admonishes, **"put on the whole armour of God** that you might be able to **stand against satanic wiles"**. There is a real devil, a real enemy roaming around seeking to devour you, to destroy you and your testimony. This is why it is so important for you to know, study and live God's Word. You must know **your adversary** the devil. The Word is your hiding place, your strong tower against the enemy; it is your rock of defense, your armour, and your safety zone.

The Apostle Paul and the disciples of old had victory over their battles and **test** because of **The Word of God, and the name of the Lord Jesus!** Jesus had victory also through the Word of God in His battles against satanic powers. "Jesus was tempted and tested as we are and yet He passed every **test"**. You can do it!

Remember, **your faith is being tried by fiery testing** in these times. These are the last days and God is yet reminding you to not think it strange when you go through your many trials, your testing (I Peter 4:12-13). **Your faith is in a fight!** The Word declares that the trials, **the testing of your faith,** and what you must go through is more precious than gold that perisheth, **"though it be tried with fire",** might be found unto **praise, honor** and **glory** at the appearing of Jesus Christ.

*Wherein ye greatly rejoice, though **now for a season,** if need be, ye are in heaviness through manifold temptations: **that the trial of your faith,** being much more precious than of gold that perisheth, **though it be tried with fire,** might be found unto praise and honour and glory at the appearing of Christ.*
                                                I Peter 1:6-7

Jesus is coming back soon, and He is looking and coming for a Church without spots, wrinkles or blemishes. The **fiery trials** and **testing** will rid us of all the impurities of sin that causes our spiritual garments to be spotted, and will produce in us love and a lifestyle of holiness which is the will of God by Christ Jesus for our lives.

Today we are in manifold temptations **(diverse testing)** and we have a lot more to endure before Christ' return but we have a way of escape. **Jesus is the way!**

We can be ready to go back with Him when He comes, **"if"** we listen to God's message through His messengers, the ministers of God, and His prophets, if we repent and turn from sin.

Remember, **"if"** shows that a condition has to be met, that **condition** is, listen, repent and turn!

Jesus taught us how to pray... "Let us not fall into temptation but deliver us from evil...Paraphrased

Matthew 6:13

..."Today" if you will hear His voice, harden not your hearts...
Hebrew 3:15

Jesus loves you!

He is coming soon, be prepared!

The Prosperity Test

*But the God of all grace, who has called us unto His eternal glory by Christ Jesus, **after you have suffered a while**, make you perfect establish, strengthen, and settle you.*

I Peter 5:10

After you have gone through some things, experienced some things and travailed through, blessings are waiting for you. Have you not noticed that your **prosperity** comes with **suffering**? Did you not know that your gain comes through your losses and God permits it? Watch this, Jesus makes it very clear...

*And Jesus answered and said, "verily I say unto you, there is **no man** that have left house, or brethren, or sisters, or fathers, or mother, or wife, or children, or lands, for My sake, and the gospel's...*
Mark 10:29

89

But he shall receive a hundredfold now in this time, houses, and brethren, and sisters, and mothers, and children, and lands, with persecutions; and in the world to come eternal life.

Mark 10:30

Your blessings and prosperity is coming but you must go through some things in this life. **Persecution** is going to come your way, **testing** is going to come and your faithfulness with God's blessings are going to be put to the **test** before or after the blessing. Remember **persecution** often times precede your blessings...

*Blessed are you when you are **persecuted** for righteousness sake...Paraphrased*

Matthew 5:10

We have tried naming and claiming **prosperity**. We have tried laying hands on it and it's mine **prosperity**. We have confessed this and tried that, but the real issue, the real truth is "you are going to go through some **trials**, tribulation, **persecution** and afflictions before your hundredfold blessings are going to manifest". No one has, or will escape **God's test!** The greatest key for **prosperity** and success is found in the book of Joshua, **"receive it"!** ...

*This book of the law shall not depart out of your mouth; but you shall **meditate therein** day and night, that you may **observe to do** according to all that is written therein: for then you shall make your way **prosperous**, and then you shall have good success. Paraphrased*

Joshua 1:8

And all of these blessings shall come on you, and overtake you "if" you hearken unto the voice of the Lord your God. There is that conditional "if" again.

Deuteronomy 28:2

God's blessings are based on your obedience to Him, be it suffering for righteousness sake, going through your fiery trials and persecution, your rejection, or whatever the **test**. You are going to receive **now** in this time, **"but with persecution."** Abraham was a man of great riches and he went through many **tests**, so did Jacob, Solomon and many other wealthy servants of old. So obey and be blessed!

You shall remember the Lord your God; for it is He that gives you power to get wealth that He may establish His covenant which He swear unto your fathers, as it is today. Paraphrased

Deuteronomy 8:18

CHAPTER VI

INTERFERING WITH PURPOSE

*And we know that **all things** work together for good, to them that love God, to them who are called according to His purpose.*

Romans 8:28

What is your purpose? Do you know that you have a purpose? Do you know that you have a calling in God? Christ had a purpose to fulfill and you have a purpose to fulfill. You are birthed in the divine purpose of God! You were born in the foreordained plan of God! You were in the mind of God before the foundations of the world.

Even before the world was made, God had already chosen us to be His through our union with Christ, so that we would be Holy and without fault before Him.

Ephesians 1:4

Because of His love God had already decided that through Jesus Christ He would make us His children – this was His pleasure and purpose. Paraphrased

Ephesians 1:5

To the praise of the glory of His grace wherein He have made us accepted in the beloved.

Ephesians 1:6

In whom also we have obtained an inheritance, being predestinated according to the purpose of Him who worketh all things after the counsel of His own will: That we should be to the praise of His glory, who first trusted in Christ.

Ephesians 1:11-12

God has made known unto us the mystery of His will, according to His good pleasure, which He hath purposed in Himself.

Ephesians 1:9

According to the eternal purpose which He purposed in Christ Jesus our Lord.

Ephesians 3:11

God created us to praise, glorify and **please Him in every area of our lives.** Therefore, we must **allow** each individual to walk through their **purpose,** through their **testing** in Christ **without interference,** and **without hindering** them. We must pray and love them through whatever their test. Think about how many you have hindered on their way to a blessing and you threw a stumbling block in their way. It is their tests. **Allow them to pass it!**

Thou art worthy, O Lord, to receive glory and honour and power: for You have created all things, and for Your pleasure they are and were created. Paraphrased

Revelation 4:11

Consider this attempt to hinder - when Christ was **led of the Holy Spirit** into the wilderness to be **tested of the devil**, satan thought to distract and hinder Him from His destiny, His purpose. Christ flowed with His **purpose,** He met His **test** head on. He did not resist the **test**! He spoke to the hindrance, the one interfering and said, "Get thee behind Me satan, you will not make a **trial** of the Lord Your God, you will not put the Lord to a **test**!" You will not hinder My purpose!

And when the devil had ended all the temptation, he departed from Him for a season.

Luke 4:13

Who's hindering you from passing your **test**? Recognize the one interfering, bless God and pass the test! When the **season** is ended, the **test** is over. You will endure another test, but not the same one if you passed. Be aware, **satan only leaves for a season**!

When your **testing** comes, know who is behind them but also know God's **purpose** for you in the test. Know who is **interfering** with God's purpose and plan for your life, who is trying to hinder you from your destiny and blessings. God said, "I know the plans that I have for you, I know the purpose and destiny that I ordained for you".

For I know the thoughts that I think toward you, saith the Lord, thoughts of peace, and not of evil, to give you an expected end.

Jeremiah 29:11

God is not against us; He is **only** against the **sin** in our lives. God hates sin! However, He loves His people and has a great plan for our lives when we obey.

94

When Jesus was giving predictions of His suffering and coming glory in Matt 16:21-24, Peter in his presumptuousness began to **interfere with the purpose** of God saying, **"be it far from Thee, Lord; this shall not happen to You".**

From that time forth began Jesus to show unto His disciples, how that He must go unto Jerusalem, and **suffer** *many things of the elders and chief priests and scribes, and be killed, and be raised again the third day. Purpose?*

Matthew 16:21

Then Peter took Him, and began to **rebuke** *Him, saying be it far from Thee, Lord: this shall not be unto Thee.*

Matthew 16:22

But He turned, and said unto Peter, **"Get thee behind Me, satan":** *you are an offense unto Me, for you do not say the things that be of God, but those that be of men. Paraphrased*

Matthew 16:23

Then said Jesus unto His disciples, **"If"** *any man will come after Me, let him* **deny himself,** *and* **take up his cross,** *and follow Me".* There is that conditional **"if"** again!

Matthew 16:24

Peter could not see or understand the purpose of Christ! We must allow each individual to walk through their **trials** and **tests** even when we don't understand them. Walk it out through Christ! Many like Peter allow the devil to use them and often **interfere** with the **purpose** that God has ordained for one's life.

We must **not allow** ourselves to cause unnecessary battles or burdens upon one another by talking about, criticizing and mistreating each other when one is going through a **test**. You don't know the purpose God has ordained for that person's life unless God divinely reveals it. Even though, Christ had revealed to Peter and the disciples that he must go this way, Peter yet allowed satan to use him, he spoke out of his flesh and not out of revelation. His mouth caused his flesh to sin. Remember Job's comforters accused and interfered with what they did not understand also!

When the Holy Spirit warned of Apostle Paul's coming **afflictions** and **testing** the disciples tried to persuade him differently, interfering with purpose. Often times, well meaning people think that they are helping but in actuality, they are interfering with the purpose that God has for your life. The disciples were not aware that they were interfering with God's plan, His will for Paul although Paul had reminded them. He reminded them as we are reminded **"many are the afflictions of the righteous but the Lord will deliver us out of them all"**. Paul was not trying to resist his sufferings but yielded to them even though, he knew that afflictions were waiting for him at Jerusalem. He persevered and endured for Christ's sake.

*And now, behold, I go bound in the spirit unto Jerusalem, not knowing the things that shall befall me there: Save that **the Holy Ghost witnessed in every city, saying that bonds and afflictions abide me.***

Acts 20:22-23

But none of these things move me, neither count I my life dear unto myself, so that I might finish my course with joy, and the ministry, which I have received of the Lord Jesus, to testify the gospel of the grace of God.

Acts: 20:24

Paul was not moved by tribulation, he was moved by revelation!

When Paul and his company had reached Caesarea, they entered into the house of Philip the Evangelist, which was one of the seven; and abode with him.

*And the same man had four **daughters**, virgins, **which did prophesy**.*

Acts 21:9

*And as we tarried there many days, there came down from Judea a certain **prophet**, named Agabus. And when he was come unto us, he took Paul's girdle, and bound his own hands and feet, and said, **"thus saith the Holy Ghost, so shall the Jews at Jerusalem bind the man that owns this girdle, and shall deliver him into the hands of the gentiles".***

Acts 21:10-11

And when we heard these things, both we, and they of that place, besought him not to go up to Jerusalem.

Acts 21:12

*Then Paul answered, what mean you to weep and to break my heart: For **I am ready not only to be bound, but also to die at Jerusalem for the name of the Lord Jesus.***

Acts 21:13

And when he would not be persuaded, we ceased, saying, "The will of the Lord be done"*...*

Acts 21:14

God is trying to bring believers, the body of Christ into that same realm of the Spirit. He is trying to teach us to pray and seek Him when we see a sister or brother going through a **trial, a test**, because we do not know what God's will is for their life. We need to learn to confess, **"the will of the Lord be done"** as we do not know what God is working in or out of their life. Job's brethren accused him when he went through his **testing**, thinking that he had sinned and brought God's judgments upon him. Peter said of Jesus when He was going through His test of preparation for the cross, **"Lord you can't do this"**! Peter was interfering with purpose, which was a hindrance, a stumbling block, an obstacle *attempting to block progress.* The disciples tried to persuade and convince Paul that he should not endure his **test after the Holy Ghost had already prepared him**.

In all of these **examples**, I am sure that they all meant well, but each **interfered** and attempted to hinder the **purpose** and **destiny** that God had ordained for each one's life.

Don't allow anyone to interfere with **God's will, purpose and plan** for your life to the point of persuading you to change or alter your course. Although **tested**, Jesus did not change or alter His course ordained by God, He was obedient in all things even to the death of the cross. **Don't allow it!** Whatever God's **test** or task is for your life, you can handle it through Christ. Don't let anyone get in your way. I believe Christ was saying to Peter, **"you are interfering, get out of My way."**

No **test has** or will come upon you that others have not endured. Know that God is faithful, He will not allow you to be tested to the point of destruction; but He will take that very **test, that very temptation, that very tribulation** and make it work for your good. Remember, **"It's only a test"**!

As it was revealed to the servant Job by faith and by revelation he realized that what he was going through was his **test**. You can have that same awareness. Job testified, "God knows the way that I take: when He has **tried** me, when He has **tested** me, I shall come forth as gold. I will be all that He would have me to be." What His soul desire, even that He will do. Paraphrased

Be encouraged all of these examples have been written for your learning.

You can do all things through Christ, He will give you the strength and grace to endure any trial, any test.

Phillipians 4:13

Jesus loves you and He is coming soon. Be ready, the "test" is just preparation!

ABOUT THE AUTHOR

In 1975 Mary R. Rogers had a visitation of the Godhead, was born again and later filled with the Holy Spirit and given a mission to spread the message of Jesus Christ. That visitation sparked a ministry that has touched and will continue to touch thousands for years to come.

The ministry of Mary R. Rogers is multi-faceted. She is the author of spiritual publications and evangelistic tracts including "God Is Shaking Everything," Why Do The Righteous Suffer," "**Denominational Barriers A Cunning Tool of The Devil**," and "A Vision That Shook My Soul" (her own personal testimony).

She has done missionary work both nationally and internationally, which includes Trinidad, and Madras, South India, where she has seen the reaping of a great harvest of souls, and planting a church in India. She was a former chaplain for the Essex County Correctional Youth Facility and has ministered as a chaplain for a number of hospitals. She continues her ministry of healing, deliverance, preaching and teaching the gospel throughout this nation and abroad.

In addition she is a teacher extraordinaire. She has led and participated in many workshops, seminars and revivals. She has a unique prophetic ministry and has come to be known as a woman to whom the Lord speaks.

She is the recipient of an Honorary Doctorate Degree from Kingsway Bible College in Des Moines, Iowa, a board member of United Christian Women's Fellowship Ministries and, an Associate Minister at the New Jerusalem Church of Chester, Chester, Pennsylvania. She is also the President of her God ordained ministry Miracle Revival Crusade Ministries, Budd Lake, New Jersey.